MACBETH

MACBETH

WILLIAM SHAKESPEARE

INTRODUCTION
BY DR CHRIS McNAB

This edition published in 2022 by Arcturus Publishing Limited
26/27 Bickels Yard, 151–153 Bermondsey Street,
London SE1 3HA

Typesetting by Sooky Choi

Cover design: Peter Ridley
Cover illustration: Peter Gray
Design: Mike Reynolds

AD008809UK

Printed in the UK

CONTENTS.

CONTENTS

INTRODUCTION

Macbeth is undoubtedly a towering work, ranking easily alongside other landmark Shakespearean tragedies such as *Hamlet, Othello* and *King Lear*, at least by evidence of the frequency of its production and its enduring popularity in academic curricula. Yet it is also something of an oddity, set apart from others in the canon.

For a start, it is short, although by no means the very shortest of Shakespeare's plays. That title is taken by the almost unknown *Double Falsehood* (acknowledging the ongoing debates about the authorship of that work), and several more popular titles – *The Comedy of Errors, A Midsummer Night's Dream, The Two Gentleman of Verona, The Tempest* and *Pericles* – also come in as fractionally shorter. But *Macbeth* still remains undeniably brisk; it can be comfortably performed in 1 hour 30 minutes, as compared to the marathon of *Hamlet*, requiring more than four hours to stage. This might seem a matter of little import, but it gains significance as we note the context. Of the plays shorter than *Macbeth*, the weighting is predominantly towards comedy, a genre that thrives on condensing laughs into as short a space as possible. But *Macbeth* is emphatic tragedy, immersing us in the purity of evil itself, once it takes hold. If anything, the compressed timeline of the play works to concentrate our focus on that evil, stripping out potential distractions such as comedic breaks and more benign philosophical rumination on life, all of which Shakespeare does masterfully in other plays. There is at times a definite feeling of plot abbreviation in *Macbeth*, with key events taking place unseen and short, breathless scenes driving the dramatic journey on at a pace bordering on uncomfortable. The violence of the play, initiated by the murder of King Duncan, begins an unstoppable snowball rolling, gathering speed as much as it increases the casualty list, the named victims including Banquo, MacDuff's wife and children and Young Siward. There is a clear sense that Scotland at large is, under Macbeth's rule, being bathed in blood.

Critics have also picked up on the fact that *Macbeth* is a play with its spotlight at full, wincing intensity on its two lead characters – Macbeth himself and his dark-hearted wife, Lady Macbeth. Of course, every play has its lead, and especially so where the title of the play is eponymous. But in *Hamlet*, for example, the lives, characterization and personal journeys of characters such as Claudius, Gertrude, Polonius and Ophelia are realized as vividly as Hamlet himself. Indeed, Hamlet's existential journey only truly makes sense when he is considered in fullest interaction with those around him. *Macbeth* also has a long secondary cast, but it feels a little opaque and of limited dimension, contributing more to advancing plot than to exploring the depths of their characters. Macbeth and Lady Macbeth, by contrast, have the very deepest corners of their hearts and mind excavated in the most painful detail. The distinction in the treatment feels deliberate. If anything, it somehow makes the moral failure of the two leads more intense and suffocating; we long to be free from the poisonous box inhabited by them, to breathe fresher air. Perhaps the secondary characters in Macbeth are there more to serve as a shadow screen, onto which the depravities of Macbeth and Lady Macbeth are projected in starkest relief.

Macbeth, it might be argued, is indeed the closest thing we get to a Shakespearean voyage into the heart of darkness, intensified formidably by its supernatural interventions (see below). But Macbeth and Lady Macbeth are by no means one-dimensional characters, pantomime villains. Rather, they are represented as terribly flawed, but fully human. What is unnerving about the play is the *believability* of murder, from initial spark of conception through final, dreadful act and on to the lifelong consequences. The study of murder is almost forensic, especially in the analysis of its motives, its performance and its psychological consequences. Take, for example, the famous passage from Act II, scene i, in which Macbeth builds up to the murder of Duncan:

> Is this a dagger which I see before me,
> The handle toward my hand? Come, let me clutch thee.
> I have thee not, and yet I see thee still.
> Art thou not, fatal vision, sensible
> To feeling as to sight? or art thou but
> Proceeding from the heat-oppressed brain?

I. i. 33–39

Not for Macbeth is the assassin's cold clarity. Rather his mind is warped by the scale of the act he is about to perform, entering a delirium in which reality itself is distorted, questioning everything, including the status of a dagger hanging in the air. Lady Macbeth is similarly contaminated by self-bought agonies of mind. In Act V, scene i, she sleepwalks under observance of her doctor and a colleague, muttering fevered thoughts:

> Out, damned spot! out, I say! One: two: why,
> then 'tis time to do't. Hell is murky. Fie, my
> lord, fie! a soldier, and afeard? What need we
> fear who knows it, when none can call our

> power to account? Yet who would have thought
> the old man to have had so much blood in him?

V. i. 39–43

The passage begins with blood and ends with blood, the horror escalating from a single 'spot' to the arterial gushings of a slaughtered man. Notably, Lady Macbeth speaks her sleepwalking visions in prose, not blank verse, robbing the speech of any semblance of poetic grandeur or harmonious rhythm.

There is also, ultimately, little sense of redemption in *Macbeth*. True, Macbeth is killed by Macduff. Lady Macbeth also dies, fading out offstage, her death reported with the suggestion that she has killed herself. There is no mourning these two characters, but neither do we find ourselves entirely reassured by the shouts of 'Hail, King of Scotland' (V. viii. 59). With the witches still out there, and humanity continuing its wrestle for power, there is little in the way of sunshine on the horizon.

Little wonder, therefore, that *Macbeth*, with its witches' spells and incantations and its vertiginous brutality, has become a superstitious theatrical performance to this day, despite its popularity. Modern actors, separated by more than four centuries from Shakespeare's time, still diligently refer to *Macbeth* as 'the Scottish play', even the utterance of its name believed to bring bad luck on a production – many actors will give whispered accounts of accidents, violence, strange malfunctions, ill spirits and various other maladies affecting productions of *Macbeth*. If lines from the play are quoted in a dressing room, the reckless actor is meant to exit the room, turn around three times, spit, swear and knock on the door to be readmitted. Another traditional way of reversing the curse of the play is to recount an equal number of lines from *A Midsummer's Night Dream*, a light comedic play whose supernatural forces are airy and humorous, rather than malign and insidious.

Having recognized the grim framework of *Macbeth*, however, we must equally now attest to its brilliance. To set the scene for this evaluation, we will first draw the lines of the plot and the characters within, illustrating how the chaos of evil is nevertheless held together in a single, unified dramatic whole.

THE PLOT

Macbeth begins in a flash and rumble of sinister disquiet, the thunder and lightning of **Act I, scene i**, appearing to fracture nature with sinister portent. We meet three witches on the blasted moorland, learning almost nothing about them (they remain unnamed throughout the play) apart from their intention to meet with Macbeth. The scene is exceptionally short – just 12 lines of speech – but the sense of foreboding is clear, reinforced by the contamination implied by the 'fog and filthy air' (I. i. 12).

Act I, scene ii, switches to a military camp where, contra the base supernaturalism of the preceding scene, we are brought into the presence of royal order, in the form of King Duncan, accompanied by his sons Malcolm and Donalbain, the thane Lennox, and various attendants. It is the aftermath of battle, and a wounded captain brings Duncan news of distant victory. Macbeth, the thane of Glamis, has defeated dual foes – a rebellion of Highlanders and Islanders and then a follow-up attack by Sweno, King of Norway. The king and his noble company laud Macbeth's valour; through the recounted story, he appears the most loyal of the king's subjects, albeit one capable of exercising extreme brutality in warfare, giving an ominous synergy with the witches' as yet unknown plans for him. Macbeth's fidelity to the royal cause, however, is most visibly contrasted with that of the Thane of Cawdor who, as reported by the Thane of Ross, attempted to swap his loyalties to the King of Norway as the battle hung in the balance. Duncan condemns Cawdor to death and passes his title to Macbeth. Duncan's final words in the scene: 'What he hath lost, noble Macbeth hath won', give a clear sense of vaunted trajectory for Macbeth – we wait to meet him in dramatic suspense.

Act I, scene iii, sees the return of the witches, at first ruminating on their ability to bring malign misfortune on distant others, specifically upon a sailor out in the Mediterranean, condemned because his wife back in England had verbally abused one of the sisters. The power they display is not that of divine fiat, but rather an ability to contaminate goodness and nature, aided by the inherent predispositions of people.

The scene shifts as we meet Macbeth for the first time, with his loyal companion, the thane Banquo. Crucially, the first line Macbeth speaks – 'So foul and fair a day I have not seen' (I. iii. 38) chimes with the witches' incantation in scene i: 'Fair is foul, and foul is fair' (I. i. 11), auguring that Macbeth's destiny is intertwining with witches' intent. The witches greet Macbeth both in the present and predictively, as Thane of Glamis, Thane of Cawdor (a promotion of which Macbeth is yet oblivious), and 'thou shalt be king hereafter' (I. iii. 50). While Banquo shows scepticism and intellectual restraint, Macbeth is clearly unsettled and energized by the possibilities of what the witches declare, especially when the third witch says to Banquo: 'Thou shalt get kings, though thou be none' (I. iii. 67). The witches quickly disappear, leaving Macbeth and Banquo pondering what they have seen. Then nobles Ross and Angus arrive, startling Macbeth by declaring that he has been made Thane of Cawdor. As the rest of the scene develops, we clearly see the beginning of Macbeth's possession by an increasingly insidious ambition, which appears both to thrill and deeply unsettle him:

> If good, why do I yield to that suggestion
> Whose horrid image doth unfix my hair
> And make my seated heart knock at my ribs,
> Against the use of nature?
>
> I. iii. 134–37

Act I, scene iv, takes us to the Scottish court, opening with Malcolm's confirmation that the traitorous former Thane of Cawdor has now been executed. Macbeth, Banquo, Ross and Angus arrive, and there is an effusive exchange of thanks and reverence between Macbeth and Duncan, the king also acknowledging Banquo, saying: 'let me infold thee / And hold thee to my heart' (I. iv. 31–32). Crucially, however, Duncan names his son Malcolm as the Prince of Cumberland, putting him next in line to the throne. For Macbeth, this is jolt, and 'a step / On which I must fall down, or else o'erleap' (I. iv. 48–49). In his alarming, dark aside, he implores that the stars hide themselves and 'Let not light see my black and deep desires' (I. iv. 51) – there is clearly a malevolent awakening.

The scene ends with the king announcing that he will travel to stay with Macbeth and his wife, and **Act I, scene v**, is our introduction to said Lady Macbeth. She is reading a letter from her husband, telling her of the strange meeting with the witches and content of their apparently prophetic visions. Lady Macbeth is as stirred by the prospect of the royal crown as her husband, and clearly conceives of Duncan's murder as the way to expedite the ascension, although she fears that her husband is 'too full o' the milk of human kindness' (I. v. 18) to perform the required deed. Yet on learning from Macbeth, who arrives at the castle, that Duncan is coming to visit, she begins to plot his murder, making alarmingly instant supplications that the dark spirits strip her of all tenderness, mercy and compassionate femininity.

A short **Act I, scene vi**, shows the arrival of Duncan and his retinue at Macbeth's castle, with Duncan exchanging with Lady Macbeth. In **Act I, scene vii**, however, Macbeth opens with a soliloquy wrestling between bloody ambition and a still-flickering flame of decency, recognizing Duncan's virtue and also that the precedent of regicide might come back to haunt him. Lady Macbeth arrives, and through steely taunts of his masculinity and the imposition of an iron focus she convinces Macbeth to go through with the plan that she has devised, to murder Duncan in his sleep and make it appear as though the guards perpetrated the crime. Macbeth consents: 'I am settled, and bend up / Each corporal agent to this terrible feat' (I. vii. 82–83).

Act II, scene i, brings the moment of action for Macbeth. Walking through the castle late at night, he meets Banquo and his son Fleance, Banquo telling Macbeth that Duncan has retired to bed. Banquo also confesses a certain disquiet: 'I dreamt last night of the three weird sisters:

/ To you they have show'd some truth' (II. i. 20–21). What this truth might be, Macbeth defers to a later discussion, and they separate. Then Macbeth hears a bell, rung by Lady Macbeth, signalling that it is time for him to perform the murder of Duncan. His overwrought mind ruminates on the vision of the dagger, and his soliloquy is pregnant with the language of symbolism of the underworld and a sense that an almost predestinate evil has taken over:

> Now o'er the one half-world
> Nature seems dead, and wicked dreams abuse
> The curtain'd sleep; witchcraft celebrates
> Pale Hecate's offerings
>
> II. i. 49–52

Act II, scene ii, brings intent to its climax. Macbeth returns to his bedchamber, covered in blood from the killing and gripping the twin daggers Lady Macbeth had left in Duncan's room, as instruments by which to blame the guards, whom Lady Macbeth has drugged insensible. Macbeth is clearly distressed psychologically and morally, stating that 'Methought I heard a voice cry "Sleep no more! / Macbeth does murder sleep"' (II. ii. 36–37). Lady Macbeth goes back to Duncan's chamber to replace the blades, then returns, watching her disintegrating husband with increasing alarm and imploring that he gain control of himself.

Act II, scene iii, has a brief moment of lighter relief, as a drunken porter answers knocking on the castle gates, although his rantings about being a porter for hell scarcely alleviate the mood. Nobles Macduff and Lennox have arrived, and the latter reflects on the menace that seems present in nature itself that night:

> The night has been unruly: where we lay,
> Our chimneys were blown down, and, as they say,
> Lamentings heard i' the air, strange screams of death
>
> II. iii. 59–61

Macduff goes to the king's room and discovers Duncan's body, and raises the alarm. The blame is placed on the guards, albeit with hints of questioning on the part of Lennox, but then Macbeth confesses that he has killed the guards in fury. Feigning innocence well, Macbeth and Lady Macbeth cry out against the injustice, Lady Macbeth fainting and being carried out. Malcolm and Donalbain secretly agree that their lives might also be in danger, so they decide to separate and leave Scotland, Malcolm going to England and Donalbain to Ireland.

Bringing the Act to a close, **Act II, scene iv**, sees Ross and an old man talking of the strange disturbances witnessed around, such as Duncan's horses killing and eating each other. Macduff enters, and acknowledges that the disappearance of Malcolm and Donalbain puts them under suspicion for the murder. Macduff also verifies that Macbeth has now gone to Scone (the place of the crowning of Scottish kings) for his coronation.

Macbeth and Lady Macbeth – now king and queen – have seen the ultimate realization of their murderous plan. What they do not have is peace. In **Act III, scene i**, Macbeth, his capacity for murder now unbottled, turns a nervous paranoia upon Banquo, remembering that the three witches had:

> ... hail'd him [Banquo] father to a line of kings:
> Upon my head they placed a fruitless crown
> And put a barren sceptre in my gripe,
> Thence to be wrench'd with an unlineal hand,
> No son of mine succeeding.
>
> III. i. 60–64

He meets with two murderers, and assigns them to kill both Banquo and Fleance, as they ride out of the castle in darkness before the banquet Macbeth and Lady Macbeth are throwing for other nobles. Macbeth's scheming belies a tormented mind. In **Act III, scene ii**, both Macbeth and Lady Macbeth reveal their stricken anguish, tormented by the moral degradation of what they have done and the lack of peace brought by the continuing need to maintain their position, the latter compelling them to further evils. 'O, full of scorpions is my mind, dear wife!' declares Macbeth (III. ii. 36). With **Act III, scene iii**, any pity we might be feeling for Macbeth is eroded by the murder of Banquo by three murderers (another killer has joined the original two, although his role seems uncertain), but Fleance escapes.

Act III, scene iv, invites us to witness a fraught banquet back at the castle, one of the murderers sneaking in to tell Macbeth that Banquo's killing has been performed. Macbeth once again seems to succumb to vibrant distress, but soon he has an embodiment of his fears, when the ghost of Banquo walks into the room and sits in Macbeth's seat, visible to no one but the king. The sight pushes Macbeth into a public display of madness as his guilt is externalized. Lady Macbeth attempts to excuse her husband to the guests, inventing a long-standing medical fit, but the worrying streams of consciousness coming from Macbeth's mouth compel her to ask her guests to leave. Once alone, Macbeth tells his wife that he is resolved to go to see the weird sisters once more, to find out for certain his destiny, and to embrace a cold-hearted focus upon his own position and survival.

A stage direction '*A heath. Thunder. Enter the three Witches, meeting*

Hecate' at the head of **Act III, scene v**, brings us back into the realm of the supernatural. The scene is a short one, but almost wholly taken by a monologue from Hecate – the goddess of witchcraft – who berates the three witches for acting against Macbeth without consulting her. Relegating them to the preparation of further spells, Hecate makes clear that she plans 'Great business' (III. iv. 22) for Macbeth, in which she shall 'draw him on to his confusion' (III. iv. 29), his downfall. While this Act shows the forces of the underworld at work, **Act III, scene vi**, depicts matters still moving in the temporal realm. Lennox speaks with another lord, expressing his suspicions of Macbeth in the murder of Duncan and Banquo, and referring to him as a 'tyrant' in the manner of his rule. The lord explains that both Malcolm and Macduff are in England raising political and military support, by which peace and order might once again be restored to Scotland.

Macbeth has now entered a new dynamic, with its titular character seeking to preserve his throne rather than gain it, perpetuating his cycle of anxiety. In Act **IV, scene i**, Macbeth once again seeks the ambiguous counsel of the witches, deep in a cavern within which the three sisters cluster around a cauldron, casting noisome spells. Macbeth, eager to displace his fears for the future, is shown three apparitions, accompanied by three prophecies – beware of Macduff; 'none of woman born / Shall harm Macbeth' (IV. i. 80–81); and he will remain safe until Birnam Wood comes to Dunsinane Hill. Macbeth takes the prophecies with hearty encouragement. But a subsequent summoned vision – a line of eight kings with Banquo's ghost following – raises again the prospect of Banquo's line becoming royally dominant. Macbeth explodes in rage, abusing the witches and resolving to massacre Macduff's entire family. It is clear that the witches' dance around the truth brings no consolation or composure to Macbeth; instead he notes that 'Infected be the air whereon they ride, / And damn'd all those that trust them!' (IV. i. 138–40). But, good to his new purpose, Macbeth commissions the killing of Lady Macduff and her son, carried out with brutality in **Act IV, Scene ii**, the tenderly playful affection between mother and son which opens the scene contrasting with the brutal manhunt subsequently unleashed upon them. Notably, Lady Macduff attacks her husband's character in an opening conversation with Ross, perceiving that he has abandoned them in Scotland while he resides in safety in England:

> He loves us not;
> He wants the natural touch: for the poor wren,
> The most diminutive of birds, will fight,
> Her young ones in her nest, against the owl.

IV. ii. 8–11

Although the following scene will show Macduff's move to England as part of a greater effort to save Scotland, Lady's Macduff's evaluation has a gut-level ring of truth about it. She stands in contrast and counterpoint to Lady Macbeth, who vilifies her husband for weakness in acting to take crown, whereas Lady Macduff reviles her husband for having the strength to put country before marriage.

Act IV, scene iii, takes us to the palace of the English king, where Malcolm meets with Macduff, the latter at first profoundly unaware that his family have just been put to the sword by Macbeth. Macduff explains the 'Great tyranny' under which Scotland has fallen, and seeks Malcolm and England's help to remove Macbeth by force from the throne. Malcolm, at first suspicious of Macduff's motives, tests him, claiming that he would be a worse, more brutal, more lascivious king than Macbeth. Macduff's measured counterarguments, however, convinces Malcolm of his trustworthiness, and he reveals the counterfeit of the test. Malcolm assures Macduff that an English army is already heading north to Scotland. Macduff's joy at this fact then undergoes precipitous collapse, as Ross arrives and, after a period of evasion, tells Macduff that his family have been massacred. Macduff collapses into grief, but on Malcolm's urging repurposes grief into anger and focused intent, specifically to kill Macbeth: 'Bring thou this fiend of Scotland and myself; / Within my sword's length set him' (IV. iii. 233–34).

The final Act of *Macbeth* now begins, the pace quickening through the structural rapidity of no fewer than eight short scenes (nine in some editions), one following quick on the heels of the other. **Act V, scene i**, brings us back into contact with Lady Macbeth, as a 'Doctor of Physic and a Waiting-Gentlewoman' observe and debate the queen's mental collapse, evinced by the madness and the truth of her sleepwalk ramblings. It is clear that scheming violence has also been Lady Macbeth's mental condemnation. In some of the last lines of the scene, however, the doctor reconnects the personal with the universal, noting that:

> Foul whisperings are abroad: unnatural deeds
> Do breed unnatural troubles: infected minds
> To their deaf pillows will discharge their secrets
>
> V. i. 79–81

Again, the word 'Foul' resonates with the supernaturalism that is abroad. There is also the language of disease – the late 1500s saw a resurgence in the plague, sweeping across England and wider Europe, so the sense of contagion would have been elevated in the contemporary audience, as would the explanation that plague was caused by God's judgement for human sin.

In **Act V, scene ii**, Scottish nobles discuss the movement of events and their part in them, intending to go to Birnam wood to join the advancing English army. They discuss Macbeth and his increasingly crumbling hold on power, his outward rule reflecting his inner disorder. The noble Angus states that:

> His secret murders sticking on his hands;
> Now minutely revolts upbraid his faith-breach;
> Those he commands move only in command,
> Nothing in love
>
> V. ii. 17–20

The point is clear – rule by fear is built on the most fragile foundations. The nobles reiterate the language of medicine and disease – 'Meet we the medicine of the sickly weal' (V. ii. 27) – giving the impression that through Macbeth Scotland has succumbed to a systemic illness that must be cured.

From second-hand accounts of Macbeth, in **Act V, scene iii**, we see him first-hand again, besieged in Dunsinane Castle. The scene opens with Macbeth's defiance, confident that the witches' prophecies mean he is beyond harm, and that he will fight on the field with impunity. His gnawing ebullience, however, has points of instability. He acknowledges that 'I have lived long enough: my way of life / Is fall'n into the sear, the yellow leaf' (V. iii. 22–23). He is also troubled by his doctor's reports of Lady Macbeth's mental health, his enquiries to the doctor implicitly revealing the diagnosis Macbeth himself knows all too well: 'Canst thou not minister to a mind diseased, / Pluck from the memory a rooted sorrow' (V. iii. 40–41). To this, the doctor replies that 'Therein the patient / Must minister to himself' (V. iii. 46–47) – in matters of self-caused mental harm, there is no cure beyond the individual's own redemption or conscience.

Act V, scenes iv and **v** advance the military action against Macbeth. In scene iv, an English army, led assuredly by Malcolm, advances on Dunsinane from Birnam wood. Malcolm orders that his soldiers cut down leafy boughs from the wood, and hold them in front as a means by which to hide their numbers from the enemy. Here the audience sees the first evidence of how the witches' prophecies to Macbeth ultimately won't protect him – now Birnam wood is coming to Dunsinane hill. Scene v flips the viewpoint to Macbeth's castle, a place of chaos and fear. After hearing a female cry out, Macbeth is informed that Lady Macbeth is dead, and there is a clear sense that she has committed suicide. The news prompts pause in Macbeth's headlong rush to war, and a deep reflection upon the way time voraciously, steadily, eats its way through human lives:

> To-morrow, and to-morrow, and to-morrow,
> Creeps in this petty pace from day to day,
> To the last syllable of recorded time;
> And all our yesterdays have lighted fools
> The way to dusty death.
>
> V. v. 19–23

Progressively, events are emptying Macbeth's life of meaning and context, and the witches' prophecies are no protection against time's depredations.

Act V, scene vi, just 10 lines long, sees the English army, drums throbbing and banners flying, throw down their branches on Malcolm's orders and launch the attack. **Act V, scene vii**, brings the first combat, and Macbeth and Young Siward (son of the Earl of Northumberland, the earl having raised the army) fighting with swords. Macbeth, confident that there is no loophole in the prophecy that he cannot be killed by anyone born of woman, fights with brio, and kills his young opponent, although Malcolm and Old Siward now enter the field of battle, Old Siward noting that: 'This way, my lord; the castle's gently render'd / The tyrant's people on both sides do fight' (V. vi. 24–25). With Macbeth's castle gone and his army starting to fragment and desert, his house of cards is beginning to topple.

Act V, scene viii, brings the final confrontation, between a vengeful Macduff and a cornered Macbeth. Macbeth taunts his opponent with the witches' prophecy, to which Macduff replies that he was born by Caesarean section, not by natural birth. A slap of realization shows Macbeth how he has been deceived by the prophecies, the deception being both the witches' plan and his own self-delusion. At first he resolves not to fight Macduff, but Macduff's wrathful promises to declare him a coward and parade him around the kingdom in ignominy compels Macbeth to return to battle. Macbeth is killed, his head severed from his body, and Malcolm and his nobles enter in victory, shouting: 'Hail, King of Scotland!' The last words of the play belong to Malcolm, who begins to set out his political reformation, declaring that thanes will now become earls and that those who have been exiled by Macbeth will be brought home.

THE HISTORICAL CONTEXT

Macbeth was written at the beginning of the seventeenth century, its first performance likely in August 1606 at the royal court, at an event to mark the visit of James I's brother-in-law, King Christian of Denmark. In all of Shakespeare's works, but especially his history plays, the time at which they were written and the sources available to Shakespeare all have a significant bearing upon the works that finally emerged. *Macbeth* is no exception.

The first point of reference is that Macbeth was an actual historical Scottish king, who reigned from 1040 until his death in August 1057. The real Macbeth did indeed come to the throne after killing Duncan I, but rather in battle near Eglin and not as a furtive murder in the king's bed. He fought a battle against rebel forces in 1045 near Dunkeld, near the village of Birnam, and the following year Siward, the Earl of Northumberland, wrestled to supplant Macbeth and install Duncan's son, Malcolm, on the throne. He failed in the attempt, but in 1054 he compelled Macbeth to relinquish territories in southern Scotland, and a final confrontation came in 1057, when Malcolm, assisted by an English army, killed Macbeth in battle. It should be noted that, contrary to Shakespeare's depiction, Macbeth was actually regarded positively as a king.

Shakespeare's primary reference work for Macbeth was the ever-popular *Chronicles of England, Scotland and Ireland*, a collective work drawn together by Raphael Holinshed and published in 1577. Holinshed (as the work is commonly known) was a key source for many of the Renaissance writers, including Marlowe, Spenser and Daniel, and Shakespeare drew on it for more than a third of his plays, including *Richard III, King Lear* and *Macbeth*. Yet Shakespeare did not slavishly copy his sources. Furthermore, his adaptations had to sit carefully astride the politics and powers of the day, which in the case of *Macbeth* meant that he had to have special regard for the new monarch, James I.

James was the only son of Mary, Queen of Scots, who had been executed in 1587 on the orders of Queen Elizabeth I. From 1567 to 1625 James ruled as the King of Scotland, as James VI, but on the death of Elizabeth he took the English crown also as James I; the two kingdoms were thereafter ruled by one monarch, the single authority eventually formalized in the Act of Union of 1707.

For the English, the de facto unification of England and Scotland under James was a matter of caution. Scotland was regarded as a bloody and unruly region, not least because of its murderous relationship to monarchs. This perceived wildness is certainly a general context in Shakespeare's *Macbeth*, which is underwritten by the need for Malcolm, with English help, to bring some order to the land north of the border. Shakespeare was nevertheless keen to modify some of the details of Holinshed for the royal eye, such as not mentioning that Sweno's army was reinforced by Danish soldiers – which would doubtless have displeased King Christian. In Holinshed, Banquo is also an accomplice to Macbeth in the murder of Duncan, rather than the guileless hero of Shakespeare's play. There was political necessity here, as James I partly rested his own right to the throne because of his descent from Banquo, as suggested in the visionary parade of kings in the play.

But *Macbeth* also struck a chord with several contemporary hot topics, not least that of regicide. On 5 November 1605 a group of British Catholics, led by one Robert Catesby, attempted to blow up James and Parliament with barrels of gunpowder placed in a cellar in the Parliament building. The plot was foiled when one of the conspirators, the legendary Guy Fawkes, whose effigy is still burned (albeit increasingly rarely) upon British bonfires to this day, was discovered lurking near the gunpowder. The events sent shockwaves through the British establishment. Some interpret *Macbeth's* Porter's reference to an 'equivocator' in Act II, Scene iii, as a reference to one of the Gunpowder Plot conspirators, Henry Garnet, who had written a treatise on the morality of equivocation.

Shakespeare, however, had to tread a fine line in his reflections upon regicide, doing so with his characteristic ambiguity. James I/VI was an intellectual at heart, and had written major treatises on the divine right of monarchs to rule – *The Trew Law of Free Monarchies* (1598) and *Basilicon Doron* (1599). In James' view a monarch, appointed directly by God, sat beyond the reproach or action of mere mortals below, even if he ruled poorly and cruelly. Indeed, he had official theological backing for this idea, in the church doctrine 'An Homily against Disobedience and Wilful Rebellion' (1571), which stated explicitly that no matter how bad the rule, rebellion was a crime of great magnitude:

> What shall Subjects do then? Shall they obey valiant, stout, wise, and good Princes [the monarch], and contemn, disobey, and rebel against children being their Princes, or against indiscreet and evil governors? God forbid: for first what a perilous thing were it to commit unto the Subjects the judgment which Prince is wise and godly, and his government good, and which is otherwise: as though the foot must judge of the head: an enterprise very heinous, and must needs breed rebellion.

Macbeth is a play explicitly about regicide. The final dethroning and killing of Macbeth flies in the face of the theories of divine right and the Homily, but it's worth noting that James, in *Basilica Doron*, drew a distinction between 'a lawfull good King and a usurping tyrant', the latter who lives 'a miserable and infamous life' and ultimately 'armeth in end his owne Subjects to become his burreaux [hangmen]'. Thus while James does not see regicide as a moral imperative, he does recognize that the quality of the king's rule has a bearing on his future. The fact that Macbeth is himself a perpetrator of the most cowardly act of regicide gives Shakespeare room to pursue Macbeth's destruction, although as a play *Macbeth* stands at an awkward angle to the belief in the divine right to rule.

WITCHES AND WITCHCRAFT

Another of James' intellectual preoccupations was the matter of witchcraft, publishing his influential work *Demonology* in 1597, which opens with an explicit declaration of his belief in witches: 'The fearefull aboundinge at this time in this countrie, of these detestable slaues of the Deuill, the Witches or enchaunters, hath moved me (beloued reader) to dispatch in post, this following treatise of mine.' James' belief in witchcraft was commonplace but not universal. One particular dissenter, mentioned with contempt in James' preface, was Sir Reginald Scot, a courtier to Queen Elizabeth. (Elizabeth herself believed in witchcraft, passing the Witchcraft Act of 1563, but was not as preoccupied about the subject as James would be.) In *The Discoverie of Witchcraft* (1584), Scot presciently argued that in most cases those accused of witchcraft were simply old and disadvantaged women who were the victims of spiteful revenge.

Macbeth embraces supernatural devilry to a heightened degree. The three witches, governed by Hecate, seem to lurk like horrifying puppet-masters in the background, casting spells and crafting malevolent outcomes like wax dolls. Certainly, the Renaissance era was a period in which belief in literal witches was a prevalent belief and fear. The death of farm animals, failure of crops and sudden illnesses or misfortunes (especially following arguments) were often blamed on the schemes of witches, who were typically identified as the marginalized, widowed and unusual women in the neighbourhood. Once accused of witchcraft, they faced a perilous future in feverish and biased courts, and after trial many were tortured or executed in horrible fashion. At a higher level, there were some much popularized cases in which it was claimed that witches were using their powers directly to threaten English monarchs.

In *Macbeth*, the actual level of power possessed by the witches is unclear. Certainly, their activity punctuates and underpins the movement of the play and the decision-making of its lead character. In Act III, scene v, Hecate berates the witches for toying with Macbeth without her involvement, and explains:

> Your vessels and your spells provide,
> Your charms and every thing beside.
> I am for the air; this night I'll spend
> Unto a dismal and a fatal end

III. v. 18–21

It is clear here that Hecate sees herself designing Macbeth's fate, giving his actions and eventual downfall an aura of evil predestination. This is constantly reinforced with frequent references to turbulent and strange forces at work in nature at large, implying that Macbeth is a focal point for malign energies far greater than he is capable of resisting.

And yet, on closer inspection, the 'metaphysical aid' (I. v. 30) of the witches, as Lady Macbeth describes it, seems less a matter of outright control than simple facilitation, the witches feeding Macbeth the triggers for behaviours that lie dormant within him anyway (see below). As Hecate says:

> He shall spurn fate, scorn death, and bear
> His hopes 'bove wisdom, grace and fear:
> And you all know security
> Is mortals' chiefest enemy.
>
> III. v. 30–33

Hecate's message is that if only Macbeth can be fooled into thinking he is a force greater than fate or even death, then the arrogance or mortals will take over quite naturally, and push him to do all manner of evil.

Shakespeare's own attitude to witchcraft is difficult to perceive in *Macbeth*. As we have seen in the case of Reginald Scot, belief in witchcraft, although widespread, was not a universal in Renaissance society. Shakespeare nevertheless incorporates witchcraft prominently into the play, but it seems impossible to say whether Shakespeare follows Scot or James in his beliefs. The witches are terrifying but ill-defined in their power or purpose. That is, in fact, their signal contribution: arguably their role, in *Macbeth* is as a dramatic intensifier, heightening the sense of evil walking the earth, leaving humans prey to feverish imaginations and unnamed disquiet.

SERVANTS OF EVIL? MACBETH AND LADY MACBETH

But apart from the witches, evil clearly has a face in *Macbeth*, in its titular character. As already noted above, Macbeth is not a cookie-cutter villain – Shakespeare rarely lets us off the hook that easily. Instead, Macbeth undergoes a descent into evil that is as much a warning to humanity as it is about the corruption of power.

From the outset of the play, Macbeth is set aside in our awareness, first by the witches' references to him in the opening scene, but then by testimony relating to his performance in battle. Macbeth is evidently a man capable of swinging the sword with great violence, as attested to by the bloodied captain recounting witnessing Macbeth in the earlier battle:

> Disdaining fortune, with his brandish'd steel
> Which smoked with bloody execution,
> Like valour's minion carved out his passage
> Till he faced the slave;
> Which ne'er shook hands, nor bade farewell to him,
> Till he unseam'd him from the nave to the chaps,
> And fix'd his head upon our battlements
>
> I. ii. 18–23

Although Macbeth's violence here is wielded in the cause of the king, the egregious nature of the slaughter still unsettles us. The sergeant further recounts that the violence seemed to 'memorize another Golgotha', the reference to the place of Christ's execution creating a tension in Macbeth's actions, hinting that they do not belong to those of a Christian warrior.

From the first moment that the witches suggest his royal ascendancy, Macbeth is a changed man. Invidious ambition emerges, channelling into increasingly irresistible thoughts of murder, emerging from dark corners of ambition and struggling for birth:

> Present fears
> Are less than horrible imaginings:
> My thought, whose murder yet is but fantastical,
> Shakes to my single state of man that function
> Is smother'd in surmise, and nothing is
> But what is not.
>
> I. iii. 137–42

Here Macbeth recoils in horror at the thought of murder, but he cannot deny the electrical surge of energy it gives him. This is the beginning. From this moment, evil has a dynamo-like drive, generating its own power and consequences and like a muscle becoming ever stronger the more it is worked, not least because that strength does bring a reward, however fleeting. For Macbeth, the step into evil is at first not inevitable, and he has moral wrestlings. He is clear-eyed about the goodness and nobility of characters such as Duncan and Banquo and the violation of natural and moral order that their murders represent. Yet Macbeth's resistance to his path is all too easily subverted by the influence and arguments of Lady Macbeth (see below), and once the first murder is committed, the die is cast.

Where *Macbeth* excels, however, is in opening the window on the psychological consequences of murder. The killing of Duncan, and of every subsequent victim, does not bring Macbeth resolution and peace of mind, but simply further agonies of guilt, paranoia, hallucination and sleepless condemnation. A.C. Bradley, in his famous work *Shakespearean Tragedy: Lectures on Hamlet, Othello, King Lear and Macbeth* (1905), perfectly captures the fractured nature of the man:

> But there is in Macbeth one marked peculiarity, the true
> apprehension of which is the key to Shakespeare's conception.
> This bold, ambitious man of action has, within certain limits,
> the imagination of a poet,—an imagination on the one hand
> extremely sensitive to impressions of a certain kind, and, on the

other, productive of violent disturbance both of mind and body. Through it he is kept in contact with supernatural impressions and is liable to supernatural fears.

Bradley 1905: 352

Bradley expresses the full depth of Macbeth as a character. Despite the excesses of his villainy, he is still believable as a human being, a fact that ultimately makes his evil all the worse. He digs his own mental grave with each new act – in the aftermath of Banquo's killing, it is transparent that each murder does not bring relief to Macbeth, but is simply the catalyst for new worries:

> Then comes my fit again: I had else been perfect,
> Whole as the marble, founded as the rock,
> As broad and general as the casing air:
> But now I am cabin'd, cribb'd, confined, bound in
> To saucy doubts and fears.

III. iv. 21–26

Being a murderer is to be in locked in, trapped inside a nightmarish world of your own making. Nor can it be stopped. Macbeth appears to reach a tipping point at which murder and violence become compulsory principles, too embedded in the reality of his life for him either to recant or to cease. Having witnessed Banquo's ghost, he does not seek absolution or reformation, but instead embraces a solipsistic darkness, having gone too far to turn back:

> For mine own good
> All causes shall give way: I am in blood
> Stepp'd in so far that, should I wade no more,
> Returning were as tedious as go o'er

III. iv. 135–38

For so much of his journey, Macbeth at least has the power of knowing that the witches have seen an impervious and great destiny for him. This knowledge provides a source of energy, powering him through to the other side of his mental decay, where he at least discovers action. Once he finally emerges into the realization that the witches' prophecies are mere equivocating illusions, his collapse is total, falling into a nihilism stripped of all religious frameworks and human dignity:

> Out, out, brief candle!

23

> Life's but a walking shadow, a poor player
> That struts and frets his hour upon the stage
> And then is heard no more: it is a tale
> Told by an idiot, full of sound and fury,
> Signifying nothing.

V. v. 23–28

The power of this well-known passage is that the theatre itself becomes a live demonstration of mortality. The temporal duration of the play becomes the ticking clock of life's end, beyond the stage as well as on it.

Macbeth is, of course, not alone in this journey. Lady Macbeth is an epic female character in the Shakespearean canon, one that many veteran female actors long to take on and interpret as their own. Her appearance in Act I, scene v, is little short of shocking. Her murderous ambition is purer and sharper than her husband's, as she fully comprehends that the plan she has hatched requires a complete reformulation of character:

> Come, you spirits
> That tend on mortal thoughts, unsex me here,
> And fill me, from the crown to the toe, top-full
> Of direst cruelty! make thick my blood,
> Stop up the access and passage to remorse,
> That no compunctious visitings of nature
> Shake my fell purpose, nor keep peace between
> The effect and it!

I. v. 41–48

Here Lady Macbeth realizes that the gentle femininity conceived by her age is useless to her purpose. She implores evil spirits to take possession of her, to transform her into pure malicious intent. Yet we have no real confirmation of whether the underworld plays any actual part in Lady Macbeth's transformation. Like her husband, there is a sense in which dark original sin is built within us all, ready to be drawn out into a dominant, active character trait should the motivation prove strong enough.

What Lady Macbeth provides to her husband is the discipline and drive he initially lacks. She wields him like a sword, drawing out mocking slanders about his masculinity to drive him on to action. The only other female frame of reference in the play is Lady Macduff, whom Shakespeare largely presents as compassionate, although she is bitter for her husband leaving them alone and vulnerable. Even this is dramatically forgiven. As a mother (Lady Macbeth is childless – her primary concern is directed to self), Lady Macduff's world is that of domesticity and her children, and she attests a shocked innocence at what is about to befall her as the murderers close in:

> I have done no harm. But I remember now
> I am in this earthly world, where to do harm
> Is often laudable, to do good sometime
> Accounted dangerous folly

IV. ii. 75–78

Lady Macbeth can make no such plea to innocence, and she knows it. In fact, both Lady Macbeth and her husband both arrive at almost an envy of the dead, who are beyond the torments the Macbeth and Lady Macbeth have inflicted upon themselves. But it soon transpires that Lady Macbeth is as undone by her actions as Macbeth himself, wracked and deranged by the sheer effort of maintaining the guilt and the schemes. A key statement comes just prior to the murder of Banquo, when she mournfully ruminates:

> Nought's had, all's spent,
> Where our desire is got without content:
> 'Tis safer to be that which we destroy
> Than by destruction dwell in doubtful joy.

III. ii. 4–7

There is an echo here of Mark 16:26: 'For what will it profit a man if he gains the whole world and forfeits his soul? Or what shall a man give in return for his soul?' Doubts are suppressed for a time, but it is noticeable in the play how Lady Macbeth, who enters as such a force of nature, progressively withers on the vine, descending into a strange sleepwalking half-creature, pitied by those who observe her, and whose death takes place without final words, or even clarity about how she has died. Evil provides a surge of energy that, once drained, becomes an entropy that reduces those it possesses to a shell.

The catharsis of *Macbeth* comes, partially, with the stillness of death once Macbeth has been killed by Macduff, and more fully in the crowning of King Malcolm. Scotland now has a virtuous and judicious ruler, the 'lawfull good King' as conceived by James I. But much lingers on after the action closes. There is no sense of the witches and their kind having been defeated – they are still out there, preying on the inconstancies and drives of nobles and subjects. There is also the disquiet about human nature itself, how quickly it can be possessed and turned, perhaps even suggested in the fact that ultimately the audience were, at least dramatically, thrilled and engrossed by a tale of murder. *Macbeth* is a play of dark hearts expressing darker actions – and turns the mirror on ourselves.

THE TRAGEDY
OF MACBETH

DRAMATIS PERSONÆ

DUNCAN, *king of Scotland.*
MALCOLM,
DONALBAIN, } *his sons.*
MACBETH,
BANQUO, } *generals of the King's army.*
MACDUFF,
LENNOX,
ROSS,
MENTEITH, } *noblemen of Scotland.*
ANGUS,
CAITHNESS,
FLEANCE, *son to Banquo*
SIWARD, *earl of Northumberland, general of the English forces.*
Young SIWARD, *his son.*
SEYTON, *an officer attending on Macbeth.*
Boy, *son to Macduff.*
An English Doctor.
A Scotch Doctor.
A Sergeant.
A Porter.
An Old Man.

Lady MACBETH.
Lady MACDUFF.
Gentlewoman attending on Lady Macbeth.

HECATE.
Three Witches.
Apparitions.

Lords, Gentlemen, Officers, Soldiers, Murderers, Attendants, and
Messengers.

SCENE: *Scotland; England.*

THE TRAGEDY
OF MACBETH

ACT FIRST

SCENE I

A desert place.

Thunder and lightning. Enter three Witches.

First Witch. When shall we three meet again
  In thunder, lightning, or in rain?

Sec. Witch. When the hurlyburly's done,
  When the battle's lost and won.

Third Witch. That will be ere the set of sun.

First Witch. Where the place?

Sec. Witch.   Upon the heath.

Third Witch. There to meet with Macbeth.

First Witch. I come, Graymalkin.

All.   Paddock calls: – anon!   10
  Fair is foul, and foul is fair.
  Hover through the fog and filthy air.

Exeunt.

SCENE II

A camp near Forres.

*Alarum within. Enter Duncan, Malcolm, Donalbain, Lennox, with
Attendants, meeting a bleeding Sergeant.*

Dun.   What bloody man is that? He can report,
    As seemeth by his plight, of the revolt
    The newest state.

Mal.   This is the sergeant
    Who like a good and hardy soldier fought
    'Gainst my captivity. Hail, brave friend!
    Say to the king the knowledge of the broil
    As thou didst leave it.

Ser.   Doubtful it stood;
    As two spent swimmers, that do cling together
    And choke their art. The merciless Macdonwald—
    Worthy to be a rebel, for to that   10
    The multiplying villanies of nature
    Do swarm upon him—from the western isles
    Of kerns and gallowglasses is supplied;
    And fortune, on his damned quarrel smiling,
    Show'd like a rebel's whore: but all's too weak:
    For brave Macbeth—well he deserves that name—
    Disdaining fortune, with his brandish'd steel
    Which smoked with bloody execution,
    Like valour's minion carved out his passage
    Till he faced the slave;   20
    Which ne'er shook hands, nor bade farewell to him,
    Till he unseam'd him from the nave to the chaps,
    And fix'd his head upon our battlements.

Dun.   O valiant cousin! worthy gentleman!

Ser.   As whence the sun 'gins his reflection
    Shipwrecking storms and direful thunders break,
    So from that spring whence comfort seem'd to come
    Discomfort swells. Mark, king of Scotland, mark:

No sooner justice had, with valour arm'd,
Compell'd these skipping kerns to trust their heels,   30
But the Norweyan lord, surveying vantage,
With furbish'd arms and new supplies of men,
Began a fresh assault.

Dun.   Dismay'd not this
Our captains, Macbeth and Banquo?

Ser.   Yes;
As sparrows eagles, or the hare the lion.
If I say sooth, I must report they were
As cannons overcharged with double cracks; so they
Doubly redoubled strokes upon the foe:
Except they meant to bathe in reeking wounds,
Or memorize another Golgotha,   40
I cannot tell—
But I am faint; my gashes cry for help.

Dun. So well thy words become thee as thy wounds;
They smack of honour both. Go get him surgeons.

Exit Sergeant, attended.

  Who comes here?

Enter Ross.

Mal.   The worthy thane of Ross.

Len. What a haste looks through his eyes! So should
   he look
That seems to speak things strange.

Ross.   God save the king!

Dun. Whence camest thou, worthy thane?

Ross.   From Fife, great king;
Where the Norweyan banners flout the sky
And fan our people cold. Norway himself   50
With terrible numbers,
Assisted by that most disloyal traitor
The thane of Cawdor, began a dismal conflict;
Till that Bellona's bridegroom, lapp'd in proof,

31

Confronted him with self-comparisons,
Point against point rebellious, arm 'gainst arm,
Curbing his lavish spirit: and, to conclude,
The victory fell on us.

Dun.   Great happiness!

Ross. That now
Sweno, the Norways' king, craves composition;
Nor would we deign him burial of his men   60
Till he disbursed, at Saint Colme's inch,
Ten thousand dollars to our general use.

Dun. No more that thane of Cawdor shall deceive
Our bosom interest: go pronounce his present death,
And with his former title greet Macbeth.

Ross. I'll see it done.

Dun What he hath lost, noble Macbeth hath won.

                              Exeunt.

SCENE III

A heath.

Thunder. Enter the three Witches.

First Witch. Where hast thou been, sister?

Sec. Witch. Killing swine.

Third Witch. Sister, where thou?

First Witch. A sailor's wife had chestnuts in her lap,
            And mounch'd, and mounch'd, and mounch'd.
            'Give me,' quoth I:
            'Aroint thee, witch!' the rump-fed ronyon cries.
            Her husband's to Aleppo gone, master o' the Tiger:
            But in a sieve I'll thither sail,

And, like a rat without a tail,
I'll do, I'll do, and I'll do.   10

Sec. Witch. I'll give thee a wind.

First Witch. Thou'rt kind.

Third Witch. And I another.

First Witch. I myself have all the other;
And the very ports they blow,
All the quarters that they know
I' the shipman's card.
I will drain him dry as hay:
Sleep shall neither night nor day
Hang upon his pent-house lid;   20
He shall live a man forbid:
Weary se'nnights nine times nine
Shall he dwindle, peak, and pine:
Though his bark cannot be lost,
Yet it shall be tempest-tost.
Look what I have.

Sec. Witch. Show me, show me.

First Witch. Here I have a pilot's thumb,
Wreck'd as homeward he did come. *Drum within.*

Third Witch. A drum, a drum!   30
Macbeth doth come.

All.   The weird sisters, hand in hand,
Posters of the sea and land,
Thus do go about, about:
Thrice to thine, and thrice to mine,
And thrice again, to make up nine.
Peace! the charm's wound up.

Enter Macbeth and Banquo.

Macb. So foul and fair a day I have not seen.

Ban. How far is't call'd to Forres? What are these
So wither'd, and so wild in their attire,   40
That look not like the inhabitants o' the earth,

33

And yet are on't? Live you? or are you aught
That man may question? You seem to understand me,
By each at once her choppy finger laying
Upon her skinny lips: you should be women,
And yet your beards forbid me to interpret
That you are so.

Macb.   Speak, if you can: what are you?

First Witch. All hail, Macbeth! hail to thee, thane of Glamis!

Sec.Witch. All hail, Macbeth! hail to thee, thane of Cawdor!

Third Witch. All hail, Macbeth, thou shalt be king hereafter!   50

Ban.   Good sir, why do you start, and seem to fear
Things that do sound so fair? I' the name of truth,
Are ye fantastical, or that indeed
Which outwardly ye show? My noble partner
You greet with present grace and great prediction
Of noble having and of royal hope,
That he seems rapt withal: to me you speak not:
If you can look into the seeds of time,
And say which grain will grow and which will not,
Speak then to me, who neither beg nor fear   60
Your favours nor your hate.

First Witch. Hail!

Sec.Witch. Hail!

Third Witch. Hail!

First Witch. Lesser than Macbeth, and greater.

Sec.Witch. Not so happy, yet much happier.

Third Witch. Thou shalt get kings, though thou be none:
        So all hail, Macbeth and Banquo!

First Witch. Banquo and Macbeth, all hail!

Macb. Stay, you imperfect speakers, tell me more: 70
        By Sinel's death I know I am thane of Glamis;
        But how of Cawdor? the thane of Cawdor lives,
        A prosperous gentleman; and to be king

Stands not within the prospect of belief,
No more than to be Cawdor. Say from whence
You owe this strange intelligence? or why
Upon this blasted heath you stop our way
With such prophetic greeting? Speak, I charge
   you.

Witches vanish.

Ban.   The earth hath bubbles as the water has,
     And these are of them: whither are they
       vanish'd?   80

Macb. Into the air, and what seem'd corporal melted
     As breath into the wind. Would they had
       stay'd!

Ban.   Were such things here as we do speak about?
     Or have we eaten on the insane root
     That takes the reason prisoner?

Macb. Your children shall be kings.

Ban.   You shall be king.

Macb. And thane of Cawdor too: went it not so?

Ban.   To the selfsame tune and words. Who's here?

Enter Ross and Angus.

Ross. The king hath happily received, Macbeth,
     The news of thy success: and when he reads   90
     Thy personal venture in the rebels' fight,
     His wonders and his praises do contend
     Which should be thine or his: silenced with that,
     In viewing o'er the rest o' the selfsame day,
     He finds thee in the stout Norweyan ranks,
     Nothing afeard of what thyself didst make,
     Strange images of death. As thick as hail
     Came post with post, and every one did bear
     Thy praises in his kingdom's great defence,
     And pour'd them down before him.

Ang.   We are sent   100
    To give thee, from our royal master, thanks;
    Only to herald thee into his sight,
    Not pay thee.

Ross. And for an earnest of a greater honour,
    He bade me, from him, call thee thane of Cawdor
    In which addition, hail, most worthy thane!
    For it is thine.

Ban.   What, can the devil speak true?

Macb. The thane of Cawdor lives: why do you dress me
    In borrow'd robes?

Ang.   Who was the thane lives yet,
    But under heavy judgement bears that life   110
    Which he deserves to lose. Whether he was combined
    With those of Norway, or did line the rebel
    With hidden help and vantage, or that with both
    He labour'd in his country's wreck, I know not;
    But treasons capital, confess'd and proved,
    Have overthrown him.

Macb. [*Aside*]   Glamis, and thane of Cawdor:
    The greatest is behind.—Thanks for your pains.—
    Do you not hope your children shall be kings,
    When those that gave the thane of Cawdor to me
    Promised no less to them?

Ban.   That, trusted home,   120
    Might yet enkindle you unto the crown,
    Besides the thane of Cawdor. But 'tis strange:
    And oftentimes, to win us to our harm,
    The instruments of darkness tell us truths,
    Win us with honest trifles, to betray's
    In deepest consequence.
    Cousins, a word, I pray you.

Macb. [*Aside*]   Two truths are told,
    As happy prologues to the swelling act
    Of the imperial theme.—I thank you,
        gentlemen.—

[*Aside*] This supernatural soliciting   130
Cannot be ill; cannot be good: if ill,
Why hath it given me earnest of success,
Commencing in a truth? I am thane of Cawdor:
If good, why do I yield to that suggestion
Whose horrid image doth unfix my hair
And make my seated heart knock at my ribs,
Against the use of nature? Present fears
Are less than horrible imaginings:
My thought, whose murder yet is but fantastical,
Shakes to my single state of man that function   140
Is smother'd in surmise, and nothing is
But what is not.

Ban.   Look, how our partner's rapt.

Macb. [*Aside*] If chance will have me king, why,
    chance may crown me,
Without my stir.

Ban.   New honours come upon him,
Like our strange garments, cleave not to their
    mould
But with the aid of use.

Macb. [*Aside*]   Come what come may,
Time and the hour runs through the roughest
    day.

Ban. Worthy Macbeth, we stay upon your leisure.

Macb. Give me your favour: my dull brain was wrought
With things forgotten. Kind gentlemen, your pains   150
Are register'd where every day I turn
The leaf to read them. Let us toward the king.
Think upon what hath chanced, and at more time,
The interim having weigh'd it, let us speak
Our free hearts each to other.

Ban.   Very gladly.

Macb. Till then, enough. Come, friends.

Exeunt.

SCENE IV

Forres. The palace.

Flourish. Enter Duncan, Malcolm, Donalbain, Lennox, and Attendants.

Dun. Is execution done on Cawdor? Are not
Those in commission yet return'd?

Mal.   My liege,
They are not yet come back. But I have spoke
With one that saw him die, who did report
That very frankly he confess'd his treasons,
Implored your highness' pardon and set forth
A deep repentance: nothing in his life
Became him like the leaving it; he died
As one that had been studied in his death,
To throw away the dearest thing he owed   10
As 'twere a careless trifle.

Dun.   There's no art
To find the mind's construction in the face:
He was a gentleman on whom I built
An absolute trust.

Enter Macbeth, Banquo, Ross, and Angus.

                                         O worthiest cousin!
The sin of my ingratitude even now
Was heavy on me: thou art so far before,
That swiftest wing of recompense is slow
To overtake thee. Would thou hadst less deserved,
That the proportion both of thanks and payment
Might have been mine! only I have left to say,   20
More is thy due than more than all can pay.

Macb. The service and the loyalty I owe,
In doing it, pays itself. Your highness' part
Is to receive our duties: and our duties
Are to your throne and state children and
          servants;
Which do but what they should, by doing every thing
Safe toward your love and honour.

Dun.   Welcome hither:
I have begun to plant thee, and will labour
To make thee full of growing. Noble Banquo,
That hast no less deserved, nor must be known   30
No less to have done so: let me infold thee
And hold thee to my heart.

Ban.   There if I grow,
The harvest is your own.

Dun.   My plenteous joys,
Wanton in fulness, seek to hide themselves
In drops of sorrow. Sons, kinsmen, thanes,
And you whose places are the nearest, know,
We will establish our estate upon
Our eldest, Malcolm, whom we name hereafter
The Prince of Cumberland: which honour must
Not unaccompanied invest him only,   40
But signs of nobleness, like stars, shall shine
On all deservers. From hence to Inverness,
And bind us further to you.

Macb. The rest is labour, which is not used for you:
I'll be myself the harbinger, and make joyful
The hearing of my wife with your approach;
So humbly take my leave.

Dun.   My worthy Cawdor!

Macb. [*Aside*] The Prince of Cumberland! that is a
            step
On which I must fall down, or else o'erleap,
For in my way it lies. Stars, hide your fires;   50
Let not light see my black and deep desires:
The eye wink at the hand; yet let that be
Which the eye fears, when it is done, to see. *Exit.*

Dun. True, worthy Banquo; he is full so valiant,
And in his commendations I am fed;
It is a banquet to me. Let's after him,
Whose care is gone before to bid us welcome:
It is a peerless kinsman.

                        Flourish. Exeunt.

SCENE V

Inverness. Macbeth's castle.

Enter Lady Macbeth, reading a letter.

Lady M. 'They met me in the day of success; and I have
learned by the perfectest report, they have
more in them than mortal knowledge. When I
burned in desire to question them further, they
made themselves air, into which they vanished.
Whiles I stood rapt in the wonder of it, came
missives from the king, who all-hailed me
'Thane of Cawdor;' by which title, before,
these weird sisters saluted me, and referred me
to the coming on of time, with 'Hail, king that   10
shalt be!' This have I thought good to deliver
thee, my dearest partner of greatness, that thou
mightst not lose the dues of rejoicing, by being
ignorant of what greatness is promised thee.
Lay it to thy heart, and farewell.'
Glamis thou art, and Cawdor, and shalt be
What thou art promised: yet do I fear thy nature;
It is too full o' the milk of human kindness
To catch the nearest way: thou wouldst be great;
Art not without ambition, but without   20
The illness should attend it: what thou wouldst
    highly,
That wouldst thou holily; wouldst not play false,
And yet wouldst wrongly win: thou'ldst have,
    great Glamis,
That which cries 'Thus thou must do, if thou have it;
And that which rather thou dost fear to do
Than wishest should be undone.' Hie thee hither,
That I may pour my spirits in thine ear,
And chastise with the valour of my tongue
All that impedes thee from the golden round,
Which fate and metaphysical aid doth seem   30
To have thee crown'd withal.

Enter a Messenger.

What is your tidings?

Mess. The king comes here to-night.

Lady M.   Thou'rt mad to say it:
Is not thy master with him? who, were't so,
Would have inform'd for preparation.

Mess. So please you, it is true: our thane is coming:
One of my fellows had the speed of him,
Who, almost dead for breath, had scarcely more
Than would make up his message.

Lady M.   Give him tending;
He brings great news. [*Exit Messenger.*]
                    The raven himself is hoarse
That croaks the fatal entrance of Duncan   40
Under my battlements. Come, you spirits
That tend on mortal thoughts, unsex me here,
And fill me, from the crown to the toe, top-full
Of direst cruelty! make thick my blood,
Stop up the access and passage to remorse,
That no compunctious visitings of nature
Shake my fell purpose, nor keep peace between
The effect and it! Come to my woman's breasts,
And take my milk for gall, you murdering
    ministers,
Wherever in your sightless substances   50
You wait on nature's mischief! Come, thick night,
And pall thee in the dunnest smoke of hell,
That my keen knife see not the wound it
    makes,
Nor heaven peep through the blanket of the dark,
To cry 'Hold, hold!'

Enter Macbeth.

                    Great Glamis! worthy Cawdor!
Greater than both, by the all-hail hereafter!
Thy letters have transported me beyond

This ignorant present, and I feel now
The future in the instant.

Macb.   My dearest love,
Duncan comes here to-night.

Lady M.   And when goes hence?   60

Macb. To-morrow, as he purposes.

Lady M.   O, never
Shall sun that morrow see!
Your face, my thane, is as a book where men
May read strange matters. To beguile the time,
Look like the time; bear welcome in your eye,
Your hand, your tongue: look like the innocent
    flower,
But be the serpent under't. He that's coming
Must be provided for: and you shall put
This night's great business into my dispatch;
Which shall to all our nights and days to come   70
Give solely sovereign sway and masterdom.

Macb. We will speak further.

Lady M.   Only look up clear;
To alter favour ever is to fear:
Leave all the rest to me.

                    Exeunt.

SCENE VI

Before Macbeth's castle.

*Hautboys and torches. Enter Duncan, Malcolm, Donalbain, Banquo,
    Lennox, Macduff, Ross, Angus, and Attendants.*

Dun.   This castle hath a pleasant seat; the air
        Nimbly and sweetly recommends itself
        Unto our gentle senses.

Ban.   This guest of summer,
The temple-haunting martlet, does approve
By his loved mansionry that the heaven's breath
Smells wooingly here: no jutty, frieze,
Buttress, nor coign of vantage, but this bird
Hath made his pendant bed and procreant
        cradle:
Where they most breed and haunt, I have
        observed
The air is delicate.

Enter Lady Macbeth.

Dun.   See, see, our honour'd hostess!   10
The love that follows us sometime is our
        trouble,
Which still we thank as love. Herein I teach you
How you shall bid God 'ild us for your pains,
And thank us for your trouble.

Lady M.   All our service
In every point twice done, and then done double,
Were poor and single business to contend
Against those honours deep and broad
        wherewith
Your majesty loads our house: for those of old,
And the late dignities heap'd up to them,
We rest your hermits.

Dun.   Where's the thane of Cawdor?   20
We coursed him at the heels, and had a purpose
To be his purveyor: but he rides well,
And his great love, sharp as his spur, hath holp
        him
To his home before us. Fair and noble hostess,
We are your guest to-night.

Lady M.   Your servants ever
Have theirs, themselves, and what is theirs, in
        compt,
To make their audit at your highness' pleasure,
Still to return your own.

Dun.   Give me your hand;
    Conduct me to mine host: we love him highly,
    And shall continue our graces towards him.   30
    By your leave, hostess.

Exeunt.

SCENE VII

Macbeth's castle.

Hautboys and torches. Enter a Sewer, and divers
Servants with dishes and service, and pass over the stage.
Then enter Macbeth.

Macb. If it were done when 'tis done, then 'twere well
    It were done quickly: if the assassination
    Could trammel up the consequence, and catch,
    With his surcease, success; that but this blow
    Might be the be-all and the end-all here,
    But here, upon this bank and shoal of time,
    We'ld jump the life to come. But in these cases
    We still have judgement here; that we but teach
    Bloody instructions, which being taught return
    To plague the inventor: this even-handed justice
    Commends the ingredients of our poison'   11
      chalice
    To our own lips. He's here in double trust:
    First, as I am his kinsman and his subject,
    Strong both against the deed; then, as his host,
    Who should against his murderer shut the door,
    Not bear the knife myself. Besides, this Duncan
    Hath borne his faculties so meek, hath been
    So clear in his great office, that his virtues
    Will plead like angels trumpet-tongued against
    The deep damnation of his taking-off;   20
    And pity, like a naked new-born babe,
    Striding the blast, or heaven's cherubin horsed
    Upon the sightless couriers of the air,
    Shall blow the horrid deed in every eye,

That tears shall drown the wind. I have no spur
To prick the sides of my intent, but only
Vaulting ambition, which o'erleaps itself
And falls on the other.

Enter Lady Macbeth.

How now! what news?

Lady M. He has almost supp'd: why have you left the
    chamber?

Macb. Hath he ask'd for me?

Lady M.   Know you not he has? 30

Macb. We will proceed no further in this business:
He hath honour'd me of late; and I have bought
Golden opinions from all sorts of people,
Which would be worn now in their newest gloss,
Not cast aside so soon.

Lady M.   Was the hope drunk
Wherein you dress'd yourself? hath it slept since?
And wakes it now, to look so green and pale
At what it did so freely? From this time
Such I account thy love. Art thou afeard
To be the same in thine own act and valour 40
As thou art in desire? Wouldst thou have that
Which thou esteem'st the ornament of life,
And live a coward in thine own esteem,
Letting 'I dare not' wait upon 'I would,'
Like the poor cat i' the adage?

Macb.   Prithee, peace:
I dare do all that may become a man;
Who dares do more is none.

Lady M.   What beast was't then
That made you break this enterprise to me?
When you durst do it, then you were a man;
And, to be more than what you were, you would 50
Be so much more the man. Nor time nor place
Did then adhere, and yet you would make both:
They have made themselves, and that their

45

fitness now
Does unmake you. I have given suck, and know
How tender 'tis to love the babe that milks me:
I would, while it was smiling in my face,
Have pluck'd my nipple from his boneless gums,
And dash'd the brains out, had I so sworn as you
Have done to this.

Macb.   If we should fail?

Lady M.   We fail!
But screw your courage to the sticking-place,   60
And we'll not fail. When Duncan is asleep—
Whereto the rather shall his day's hard journey
Soundly invite him—his two chamberlains
Will I with wine and wassail so convince,
That memory, the warder of the brain,
Shall be a fume, and the receipt of reason
A limbec only: when in swinish sleep
Their drenched natures lie as in a death,
What cannot you and I perform upon
The unguarded Duncan? what not put upon   70
His spongy officers, who shall bear the guilt
Of our great quell?

Macb.   Bring forth men-children only;
For thy undaunted mettle should compose
Nothing but males. Will it not be received,
When we have mark'd with blood those sleepy
      two
Of his own chamber, and used their very daggers,
That they have done't?

Lady M.   Who dares receive it other,
As we shall make our griefs and clamour roar
Upon his death?

Macb.   I am settled, and bend up
Each corporal agent to this terrible feat.   80
Away, and mock the time with fairest show:
False face must hide what the false heart doth
      know.

Exeunt.

ACT SECOND

SCENE I

Inverness. Court of Macbeth's castle.

Enter Banquo, and Fleance bearing a torch before him.

Ban. How goes the night, boy?

Fle. The moon is down; I have not heard the clock.

Ban. And she goes down at twelve.

Fle.   I take't, 'tis later, sir.

Ban. Hold, take my sword. There's husbandry in
            heaven,
         Their candles are all out. Take thee that too.
         A heavy summons lies like lead upon me,
         And yet I would not sleep. Merciful powers,
         Restrain in me the cursed thoughts that nature
         Gives way to in repose!

Enter Macbeth, and a Servant with a torch.

                                 Give me my sword.
            Who's there?   10

Macb. A friend.

Ban. What, sir, not yet at rest? The king's a-bed:
         He hath been in unusual pleasure, and
         Sent forth great largess to your offices:
         This diamond he greets your wife withal,
         By the name of most kind hostess; and shut up
         In measureless content.

Macb.   Being unprepared,
         Our will became the servant to defect,
         Which else should free have wrought.

Ban.   All's well.
         I dreamt last night of the three weird sisters: 20
         To you they have show'd some truth.

47

Macb.   I think not of them:
Yet, when we can entreat an hour to serve,
We would spend it in some words upon that business,
If you would grant the time.

Ban.   At your kind'st leisure

Macb. If you shall cleave to my consent, when 'tis,
It shall make honour for you.

Ban.   So I lose none
In seeking to augment it, but still keep
My bosom franchised and allegiance clear,
I shall be counsell'd.

Macb.   Good repose the while!

Ban. Thanks, sir: the like to you!   30

Exeunt Banquo and Fleance.

Macb. Go bid thy mistress, when my drink is ready,
She strike upon the bell. Get thee to bed.

Exit Servant.

       Is this a dagger which I see before me,
       The handle toward my hand? Come, let me
          clutch thee.
       I have thee not, and yet I see thee still.
       Art thou not, fatal vision, sensible
       To feeling as to sight? or art thou but
       A dagger of the mind, a false creation,
       Proceeding from the heat-oppressed brain?
       I see thee yet, in form as palpable   40
       As this which now I draw.
       Thou marshall'st me the way that I was going;
       And such an instrument I was to use.
       Mine eyes are made the fools o' the other senses,
       Or else worth all the rest: I see thee still;
       And on thy blade and dudgeon gouts of blood,
       Which was not so before. There's no such thing:
       It is the bloody business which informs
       Thus to mine eyes. Now o'er the one half-world

Nature seems dead, and wicked dreams abuse   50
The curtain'd sleep; witchcraft celebrates
Pale Hecate's offerings; and wither'd murder,
Alarum'd by his sentinel, the wolf,
Whose howl's his watch, thus with his stealthy pace,
With Tarquin's ravishing strides, towards his design
Moves like a ghost. Thou sure and firm-set earth,
Hear not my steps, which way they walk, for fear
Thy very stones prate of my whereabout,
And take the present horror from the time,
Which now suits with it. Whiles I threat, he lives: 60
Words to the heat of deeds too cold breath gives.

A bell rings.

I go, and it is done: the bell invites me.
Hear it not, Duncan, for it is a knell
That summons thee to heaven, or to hell.

Exit.

SCENE II

The same.

Enter Lady Macbeth.

Lady M. That which hath made them drunk hath made
me bold;
What hath quench'd them hath given me fire.
Hark! Peace!
It was the owl that shriek'd, the fatal bellman,
Which gives the stern'st good-night. He is about it:
The doors are open, and the surfeited grooms
Do mock their charge with snores: I have
drugg'd their possets,
That death and nature do contend about them,
Whether they live or die.

Macb. [*Within*]   Who's there? what, ho!

Lady M. Alack, I am afraid they have awaked   10
    And 'tis not done: the attempt and not the deed
    Confounds us. Hark! I laid their daggers ready;
    He could not miss 'em. Had he not resembled
    My father as he slept, I had done't.

Enter Macbeth.

              My husband!

Macb. I have done the deed. Didst thou not hear a noise?

Lady M. I heard the owl scream and the crickets cry.
    Did not you speak?

Macb.   When?

Lady M.   Now.

Macb.   As I descended?

Lady M. Ay.

Macb. Hark!
    Who lies i' the second chamber?

Lady M.   Donalbain.   20

Macb. This is a sorry sight. *Looking on his hands.*

Lady M. A foolish thought, to say a sorry sight.

Macb. There's one did laugh in's sleep, and one cried 'Murder!'
    That they did wake each other: I stood and heard them:
    But they did say their prayers, and address'd them
    Again to sleep.

Lady M.   There are two lodged together.

Macb. One cried 'God bless us!' and 'Amen' the other,
    As they had seen me with these hangman's hands:
    Listening their fear, I could not say 'Amen,'
    When they did say 'God bless us!'

Lady M.   Consider it not so deeply.   30

Macb. But wherefore could not I pronounce 'Amen'?
    I had most need of blessing, and 'Amen'
    Stuck in my throat.

Lady M.   These deeds must not be thought
       After these ways; so, it will make us mad.

Macb. Methought I heard a voice cry 'Sleep no more!
       Macbeth does murder sleep'—the innocent sleep,
       Sleep that knits up the ravell'd sleave of care,
       The death of each day's life, sore labour's bath,
       Balm of hurt minds, great nature's second course,
       Chief nourisher in life's feast,—

Lady M.   What do you mean?   40

Macb. Still it cried 'Sleep no more!' to all the house:
       'Glamis hath murder'd sleep, and therefore Cawdor
       Shall sleep no more: Macbeth shall sleep no more.'

Lady M. Who was it that thus cried? Why, worthy thane,
       You do unbend your noble strength, to think
       So brainsickly of things. Go get some water,
       And wash this filthy witness from your hand.
       Why did you bring these daggers from the place?
       They must lie there: go carry them, and smear
       The sleepy grooms with blood.

Macb.   I'll go no more: 50
       I am afraid to think what I have done;
       Look on't again I dare not.

Lady M.   Infirm of purpose!
       Give me the daggers: the sleeping and the dead
       Are but as pictures: 'tis the eye of childhood
       That fears a painted devil. If he do bleed,
       I'll gild the faces of the grooms withal,
       For it must seem their guilt.

Exit. Knocking within.

Macb.   Whence is that knocking?
       How is't with me, when every noise appals me?
       What hands are here? ha! they pluck out mine
             eyes!
       Will all great Neptune's ocean wash this blood   60
       Clean from my hand? No; this my hand will rather

        The multitudinous seas incarnadine,
        Making the green one red.

Re-enter Lady Macbeth.

Lady M. My hands are of your colour, but I shame
        To wear a heart so white. [*Knocking within.*]
        I hear a knocking
        At the south entry: retire we to our chamber:
        A little water clears us of this deed:
        How easy is it then! Your constancy
        Hath left you unattended. [*Knocking within.*]
           Hark! more knocking:
        Get on your nightgown, lest occasion call us   70
        And show us to be watchers: be not lost
        So poorly in your thoughts.

Macb. To know my deed, 'twere best not know
        myself.

Knocking within.

        Wake Duncan with thy knocking! I would thou
        couldst!

Exeunt.

SCENE III

The same.

Enter a Porter. Knocking within.

Porter. Here's a knocking indeed! If a man were porter
        of hell-gate, he should have old turning the
        key. [*Knocking within.*] Knock, knock, knock!
        Who's there, i' the name of Beelzebub? Here's a
        farmer, that hanged himself on th' expectation
        of plenty: come in time; have napkins enow
        about you; here you'll sweat for't. [*Knocking*

within.] Knock, knock! Who's there, in th'
other devil's name? Faith, here's an equivocator,
that could swear in both the scales against   10
either scale; who committed treason enough
for God's sake, yet could not equivocate to
heaven: O, come in, equivocator. [*Knocking
within.*] Knock, knock, knock! Who's there?
Faith, here's an English tailor come hither, for
stealing out of a French hose: come in, tailor;
here you may roast your goose. [*Knocking
within.*] Knock, knock; never at quiet! What
are you? But this place is too cold for hell. I'll
devil-porter it no further: I had thought to   20
have let in some of all professions, that go the
primrose way to the everlasting bonfire.
[*Knocking within.*] Anon, anon! I pray you,
remember the porter.

Opens the gate.

Enter Macduff and Lennox.

Macd. Was it so late, friend, ere you went to bed,
That you do lie so late?

Port. Faith, sir, we were carousing till the second
cock: and drink, sir, is a great provoker of
three things.

Macd. What three things does drink especially
provoke?   30

Port. Marry, sir, nose-painting, sleep and urine.
Lechery, sir, it provokes and unprovokes; it
provokes the desire, but it takes away the
performance: therefore much drink may be said
to be an equivocator with lechery: it makes
him and it mars him; it sets him on and it
takes him off; it persuades him and disheartens
him; makes him stand to and not stand to; in
conclusion, equivocates him in a sleep, and
giving him the lie, leaves him.   40

Macd. I believe drink gave thee the lie last night.

Port. That it did, sir, i' the very throat on me: but
I requited him for his lie, and, I think, being
too strong for him, though he took up my leg
sometime, yet I made a shift to cast him.

Macd. Is thy master stirring?

Enter Macbeth.

Our knocking has awaked him; here he comes.

Len. Good morrow, noble sir.

Macb. Good morrow, both.

Macd. Is the king stirring, worthy thane?

Macb. Not yet. 50

Macd. He did command me to call timely on him:
I had almost slipp'd the hour.

Macb. I'll bring you to him.

Macd. I know this is a joyful trouble to you;
But yet 'tis one.

Macb. The labour we delight in physics pain.
This is the door.

Macd. I'll make so bold to call,
For 'tis my limited service. *Exit.*

Len. Goes the king hence to-day?

Macb. He does: he did appoint so.

Len. The night has been unruly: where we lay,
Our chimneys were blown down, and, as they
say, 60
Lamentings heard i' the air, strange screams of
death,
And prophesying with accents terrible
Of dire combustion and confused events
New hatch'd to the woful time: the obscure bird

Clamour'd the livelong night: some say, the earth
Was feverous and did shake.

Macb.   'Twas a rough night.

Len.   My young remembrance cannot parallel
A fellow to it.

Re-enter Macduff.

Macd. O horror, horror, horror! Tongue nor heart
Cannot conceive nor name thee.

Macb. ⎱
Len. ⎰   What's the matter?   70

Macd. Confusion now hath made his masterpiece.
Most sacrilegious murder hath broke ope
The Lord's anointed temple, and stole thence
The life o' the building.

Macb.   What is't you say? the life?

Len.   Mean you his majesty?

Macd. Approach the chamber, and destroy your sight
With a new Gorgon: do not bid me speak;
See, and then speak yourselves.

Exeunt Macbeth and Lennox.

                              Awake, awake!
Ring the alarum-bell. Murder and treason!
Banquo and Donalbain! Malcolm! awake!   80
Shake off this downy sleep, death's counterfeit,
And look on death itself! up, up, and see
The great doom's image! Malcolm! Banquo!
As from your graves rise up, and walk like
    sprites,
To countenance this horror. Ring the bell.

Bell rings.

Enter Lady Macbeth.

Lady M. What's the business,
   That such a hideous trumpet calls to parley
   The sleepers of the house? speak, speak!

Macd.   O gentle lady,
   'Tis not for you to hear what I can speak:
   The repetition, in a woman's ear,   90
   Would murder as it fell.

Enter Banquo.

         O Banquo, Banquo!
   Our royal master's murder'd.

Lady M.   Woe, alas!
   What, in our house?

Ban.   Too cruel any where.
   Dear Duff, I prithee, contradict thyself,
   And say it is not so.

Re-enter Macbeth and Lennox, with Ross.

Macb. Had I but died an hour before this chance,
   I had lived a blessed time; for from this instant
   There's nothing serious in mortality:
   All is but toys: renown and grace is dead;
   The wine of life is drawn, and the mere lees   100
   Is left this vault to brag of.

Enter Malcolm and Donalbain.

Don. What is amiss?

Macb.   You are, and do not know't:
   The spring, the head, the fountain of your blood
   Is stopp'd; the very source of it is stopp'd.

Macd. Your royal father's murder'd.

Mal.   O, by whom?

Len. Those of his chamber, as it seem'd, had done't:
   Their hands and faces were all badged with
     blood;
   So were their daggers, which unwiped we found

Upon their pillows:
They stared, and were distracted; no man's life   110
Was to be trusted with them.

Macb. O, yet I do repent me of my fury,
That I did kill them.

Macd.   Wherefore did you so?

Macb. Who can be wise, amazed, temperate and furious,
Loyal and neutral, in a moment? No man:
The expedition of my violent love
Outrun the pauser reason. Here lay Duncan,
His silver skin laced with his golden blood,
And his gash'd stabs look'd like a breach in
    nature
For ruin's wasteful entrance: there, the murderers,   120
Steep'd in the colours of their trade, their daggers
Unmannerly breech'd with gore: who could
    refrain,
That had a heart to love, and in that heart
Courage to make's love known?

Lady M.   Help me hence, ho!

Macd. Look to the lady.

Mal. [*Aside to Don.*]   Why do we hold our tongues,
That most may claim this argument for ours?

Don. [*Aside to Mal.*] What should be spoken here,
    where our fate,
Hid in an auger-hole, may rush, and seize us?
Let's away;
Our tears are not yet brew'd.

Mal. [*Aside to Don.*]   Nor our strong sorrow   130
Upon the foot of motion.

Ban.   Look to the lady:

Lady Macbeth is carried out.

And when we have our naked frailties hid,
That suffer in exposure, let us meet,

And question this most bloody piece of work,
To know it further. Fears and scruples shake us:
In the great hand of God I stand, and thence
Against the undivulged pretence I fight
Of treasonous malice.

Macd.   And so do I.

All.   So all.

Macb. Let's briefly put on manly readiness,
And meet i' the hall together.

All.   Well contented.   140

Exeunt all but Malcolm and Donalbain.

Mal. What will you do? Let's not consort with them:
To show an unfelt sorrow is an office
Which the false man does easy. I'll to England.

Don. To Ireland, I; our separated fortune
Shall keep us both the safer: where we are
There's daggers in men's smiles: the near in blood,
The nearer bloody.

Mal.   This murderous shaft that's shot
Hath not yet lighted, and our safest way
Is to avoid the aim. Therefore to horse;
And let us not be dainty of leave-taking,   150
But shift away: there's warrant in that theft
Which steals itself when there's no mercy left.

Exeunt.

SCENE IV

Outside Macbeth's castle.

Enter Ross with an old Man.

Old M. Threescore and ten I can remember well:

Within the volume of which time I have seen
Hours dreadful and things strange, but this
  sore night
Hath trifled former knowings.

Ross.   Ah, good father,
Thou seest, the heavens, as troubled with man's
  act,
Threaten his bloody stage: by the clock 'tis day,
And yet dark night strangles the travelling
  lamp:
Is't night's predominance, or the day's shame,
That darkness does the face of earth entomb,
When living light should kiss it?

Old M.   'Tis unnatural,   10
Even like the deed that's done. On Tuesday last
A falcon towering in her pride of place
Was by a mousing owl hawk'd at and kill'd.

Ross. And Duncan's horses—a thing most strange
  and certain—
Beauteous and swift, the minions of their race,
Turn'd wild in nature, broke their stalls, flung
  out,
Contending 'gainst obedience, as they would
  make
War with mankind.

Old M.   'Tis said they eat each other.

Ross. They did so, to the amazement of mine eyes,
That look'd upon't.

Enter Macduff.

        Here comes the good Macduff.   20
How goes the world, sir, now?

Macd.   Why, see you not?

Ross. Is't known who did this more than bloody
  deed?

Macd. Those that Macbeth hath slain.

Ross.   Alas, the day!
What good could they pretend?

Macd.   They were suborn'd:
Malcolm and Donalbain, the king's two sons,
Are stol'n away and fled, which puts upon them
Suspicion of the deed.

Ross.   'Gainst nature still:
Thriftless ambition, that wilt ravin up
Thine own life's means! Then 'tis most like
The sovereignty will fall upon Macbeth.   30

Macd. He is already named, and gone to Scone
To be invested.

Ross.   Where is Duncan's body?

Macd. Carried to Colme-kill,
The sacred storehouse of his predecessors
And guardian of their bones.

Ross.   Will you to Scone?

Macd. No, cousin, I'll to Fife.

Ross.   Well, I will thither.

Macd. Well, may you see things well done there: adieu!
Lest our old robes sit easier than our new!

Ross. Farewell, father.

Old M. God's benison go with you, and with those   40
That would make good of bad and friends of foes!

Exeunt.

ACT THIRD
SCENE I

Forres. The palace.

Enter Banquo.

Ban. Thou hast it now: king, Cawdor, Glamis, all,
As the weird women promised, and I fear
Thou play'dst most foully for't: yet it was said
It should not stand in thy posterity,
But that myself should be the root and father
Of many kings. If there come truth from them—
As upon thee, Macbeth, their speeches shine—
Why, by the verities on thee made good,
May they not be my oracles as well
And set me up in hope? But hush, no more.   10

Sennet sounded. Enter Macbeth, as king; Lady Macbeth, as queen;
Lennox, Ross, Lords, Ladies, and Attendants.

Macb. Here's our chief guest.

Lady M.   If he had been forgotten,
It had been as a gap in our great feast,
And all-thing unbecoming.

Macb. To-night we hold a solemn supper, sir,
And I'll request your presence.

Ban.   Let your highness
Command upon me, to the which my duties
Are with a most indissoluble tie
For ever knit.

Macb. Ride you this afternoon?

Ban. Ay, my good lord.   20

Macb. We should have else desired your good advice,
Which still hath been both grave and prosperous,
In this day's council; but we'll take to-morrow.
Is't far you ride?

Ban. As far, my lord, as will fill up the time
'Twixt this and supper: go not my horse the better,
I must become a borrower of the night
For a dark hour or twain.

Macb.   Fail not our feast.

Ban. My lord, I will not.

Macb. We hear our bloody cousins are bestow'd   30
In England and in Ireland, not confessing
Their cruel parricide, filling their hearers
With strange invention: but of that to-morrow,
When therewithal we shall have cause of state
Craving us jointly. Hie you to horse: adieu,
Till you return at night. Goes Fleance with you?

Ban. Ay, my good lord: our time does call upon's.

Macb. I wish your horses swift and sure of foot,
And so I do commend you to their backs.
Farewell. [*Exit Banquo.*]   40
Let every man be master of his time
Till seven at night; to make society
The sweeter welcome, we will keep ourself
Till supper-time alone: while then, God be
        with you!

Exeunt all but Macbeth and an Attendant.

Sirrah, a word with you: attend those men
Our pleasure?

Attend. They are, my lord, without the palace-gate.

Macb. Bring them before us. [*Exit Attendant.*]
                                To be thus is nothing;
But to be safely thus: our fears in Banquo
Stick deep; and in his royalty of nature   50
Reigns that which would be fear'd: 'tis much he
        dares,
And, to that dauntless temper of his mind,
He hath a wisdom that doth guide his valour
To act in safety. There is none but he

Whose being I do fear: and under him
My Genius is rebuked, as it is said
Mark Antony's was by Cæsar. He chid the sisters,
When first they put the name of king upon me,
And bade them speak to him; then prophet-like
They hail'd him father to a line of kings: 60
Upon my head they placed a fruitless crown
And put a barren sceptre in my gripe,
Thence to be wrench'd with an unlineal hand,
No son of mine succeeding. If't be so,
For Banquo's issue have I filed my mind;
For them the gracious Duncan have I murder'd;
Put rancours in the vessel of my peace
Only for them, and mine eternal jewel
Given to the common enemy of man,
To make them kings, the seed of Banquo kings!   70
Rather than so, come, fate, into the list,
And champion me to the utterance! Who's there?

Re-enter Attendant, with two Murderers.

Now go to the door, and stay there till we call.

Exit Attendant.

Was it not yesterday we spoke together?

First Mur. It was, so please your highness.

Macb.   Well then, now
Have you consider'd of my speeches? Know
That it was he in the times past which held you
So under fortune, which you thought had been
Our innocent self: this I made good to you
In our last conference; pass'd in probation with
      you,   80.
How you were borne in hand, how cross'd, the
instruments,
Who wrought with them, and all things else
      that might
To half a soul and to a notion crazed
Say 'Thus did Banquo.'

First Mur.   You made it known to us.

Macb. I did so; and went further, which is now
Our point of second meeting. Do you find
Your patience so predominant in your nature,
That you can let this go? Are you so gospell'd,
To pray for this good man and for his issue,
Whose heavy hand hath bow'd you to the grave   90
And beggar'd yours for ever?

First Mur.   We are men, my liege.

Macb. Ay, in the catalogue ye go for men;
As hounds and greyhounds, mongrels, spaniels,
    curs,
Shoughs, water-rugs and demi-wolves, are clept
All by the name of dogs: the valued file
Distinguishes the swift, the slow, the subtle,
The housekeeper, the hunter, every one
According to the gift which bounteous nature
Hath in him closed, whereby he does receive
Particular addition, from the bill   100
That writes them all alike: and so of men.
Now if you have a station in the file,
Not i' the worst rank of manhood, say it,
And I will put that business in your bosoms
Whose execution takes your enemy off,
Grapples you to the heart and love of us,
Who wear our health but sickly in his life,
Which in his death were perfect.

Sec. Mur.   I am one, my liege,
Whom the vile blows and buffets of the world
Have so incensed that I am reckless what   110
I do to spite the world.

First Mur.   And I another
So weary with disasters, tugg'd with fortune,
That I would set my life on any chance,
To mend it or be rid on't.

Macb.   Both of you
Know Banquo was your enemy.

Both Mur.   True, my lord.

Macb. So is he mine, and in such bloody distance
  That every minute of his being thrusts
  Against my near'st of life: and though I could
  With barefaced power sweep him from my sight
  And bid my will avouch it, yet I must not,   120
  For certain friends that are both his and mine,
  Whose loves I may not drop, but wail his fall
  Who I myself struck down: and thence it is
  That I to your assistance do make love,
  Masking the business from the common eye
  For sundry weighty reasons.

Sec. Mur.   We shall, my lord,
  Perform what you command us.

First Mur.   Though our lives—

Macb. Your spirits shine through you. Within this
   hour at most
  I will advise you where to plant yourselves,
  Acquaint you with the perfect spy o' the time,   130
  The moment on't; for't must be done to-night,
  And something from the palace; always
   thought
  That I require a clearness: and with him—
  To leave no rubs nor botches in the work—
  Fleance his son, that keeps him company,
  Whose absence is no less material to me
  Than is his father's, must embrace the fate
  Of that dark hour. Resolve yourselves apart:
  I'll come to you anon.

Both Mur.   We are resolved, my lord.

Macb. I'll call upon you straight: abide within.   140

Exeunt Murderers.

  It is concluded: Banquo thy soul's flight,
  If it find heaven, must find it out to-night.

         Exit.

SCENE II

The palace.

Enter Lady Macbeth and a Servant.

Lady M. Is Banquo gone from court?

Serv. Ay, madam, but returns again to-night.

Lady M. Say to the king, I would attend his leisure
   For a few words.

Serv.   Madam, I will. *Exit.*

Lady M.   Nought's had, all's spent,
   Where our desire is got without content:
   'Tis safer to be that which we destroy
   Than by destruction dwell in doubtful joy.

Enter Macbeth.

   How now, my lord! why do you keep alone,
   Of sorriest fancies your companions making;
   Using those thoughts which should indeed have
      died   10
   With them they think on? Things without all
      remedy
   Should be without regard: what's done is done.

Macb. We have scotch'd the snake, not kill'd it:
   She'll close and be herself, whilst our poor malice
   Remains in danger of her former tooth.
   But let the frame of things disjoint, both the
      worlds suffer,
   Ere we will eat our meal in fear, and sleep
   In the affliction of these terrible dreams
   That shake us nightly: better be with the dead,
   Whom we, to gain our peace, have sent to peace,   20
   Than on the torture of the mind to lie
   In restless ecstasy. Duncan is in his grave;
   After life's fitful fever he sleeps well;

66

Treason has done his worst: nor steel, nor poison,
Malice domestic, foreign levy, nothing,
Can touch him further.

Lady M.   Come on;
Gentle my lord, sleek o'er your rugged looks;
Be bright and jovial among your guests to-night.

Macb. So shall I, love; and so, I pray, be you:
Let your remembrance apply to Banquo;   30
Present him eminence, both with eye and tongue:
Unsafe the while, that we
Must lave our honours in these flattering streams,
And make our faces visards to our hearts,
Disguising what they are.

Lady M.   You must leave this.

Macb. O, full of scorpions is my mind, dear wife!
Thou know'st that Banquo, and his Fleance, 'lives.

Lady M. But in them nature's copy's not eterne.

Macb. There's comfort yet; they are assailable;
Then be thou jocund: ere the bat hath flown   40
His cloister'd flight; ere to black Hecate's summons
The shard-borne beetle with his drowsy hums
Hath rung night's yawning peal, there shall be
    done
A deed of dreadful note.

Lady M.   What's to be done?

Macb. Be innocent of the knowledge, dearest chuck,
Till thou applaud the deed. Come, seeling night,
Scarf up the tender eye of pitiful day,
And with thy bloody and invisible hand
Cancel and tear to pieces that great bond
Which keeps me pale! Light thickens, and the
    crow   50
Makes wing to the rooky wood:
Good things of day begin to droop and drowse,
Whiles night's black agents to their preys do rouse.
Thou marvell'st at my words: but hold thee still;

Things bad begun make strong themselves by ill:
So, prithee, go with me.

Exeunt.

SCENE III

A park near the palace.

Enter three Murderers.

First Mur. But who did bid thee join with us?

Third Mur. Macbeth.

Sec.
Mur. He needs not our mistrust; since he delivers
Our offices, and what we have to do,
To the direction just.

First Mur. Then stand with us.
The west yet glimmers with some streaks of day:
Now spurs the lated traveller apace
To gain the timely inn, and near approaches
The subject of our watch.

Third Mur. Hark! I hear horses.

Ban. [*Within*] Give us a light there, ho!

Sec. Mur. Then 'tis he: the rest
That are within the note of expectation   10
Already are i' the court.

First Mur. His horses go about.

Third Mur. Almost a mile: but he does usually—
So all men do—from hence to the palace gate
Make it their walk.

Sec. Mur. A light, a light!

Enter Banquo, and Fleance with a torch.

Third Mur.   'Tis he.

First Mur. Stand to't.

Ban.   It will be rain to-night.

First Mur.   Let it come down.

They set upon Banquo.

Ban.   O, treachery! Fly, good Fleance, fly, fly, fly!
       Thou mayst revenge. O slave!

Dies. Fleance escapes.

Third Mur. Who did strike out the light?

First Mur.   Was't not the way?

Third Mur. There's but one down; the son is fled.

Sec. Mur.   We have lost   20
       Best half of our affair.

First Mur. Well, let's away and say how much is done.

Exeunt.

SCENE IV

Hall in the palace.

A banquet prepared. Enter Macbeth, Lady Macbeth, Ross, Lennox,
Lords, and Attendants.

Macb. You know your own degrees; sit down: at first
     And last a hearty welcome.

Lords.   Thanks to your majesty.

Macb. Ourself will mingle with society
     And play the humble host.
     Our hostess keeps her state, but in best time
     We will require her welcome.

Lady M. Pronounce it for me, sir, to all our friends,
    For my heart speaks they are welcome.

Enter first Murderer to the door.

Macb. See, they encounter thee with their hearts' thanks.
    Both sides are even: here I'll sit i' the midst: 10
    Be large in mirth; anon we'll drink a measure
    The table round. [*Approaching the door*] There's
    blood upon thy face.

Mur. 'Tis Banquo's then.

Macb. 'Tis better thee without than he within.
    Is he dispatch'd?

Mur. My lord, his throat is cut; that I did for him.

Macb. Thou art the best o' the cut-throats: yet he's
      good
    That did the like for Fleance: if thou didst it,
    Thou art the nonpareil.

Mur.   Most royal sir,
    Fleance is 'scaped.   20

Macb. [*Aside*] Then comes my fit again: I had else
      been perfect,
    Whole as the marble, founded as the rock,
    As broad and general as the casing air:
    But now I am cabin'd, cribb'd, confined, bound in
    To saucy doubts and fears.—But Banquo's safe?

Mur. Ay, my good lord: safe in a ditch he bides,
    With twenty trenched gashes on his head;
    The least a death to nature.

Macb.   Thanks for that.
    [*Aside*] There the grown serpent lies; the worm
      that's fled
    Hath nature that in time will venom breed,   30
    No teeth for the present. Get thee gone:
      to-morrow
    We'll hear ourselves again. *Exit Murderer.*

Lady M.   My royal lord,
  You do not give the cheer: the feast is sold
  That is not often vouch'd, while 'tis a-making,
  'Tis given with welcome: to feed were best at
      home;
  From thence the sauce to meat is ceremony;
  Meeting were bare without it.

Macb.   Sweet remembrancer!
  Now good digestion wait on appetite,
  And health on both!

Len.   May't please your highness sit.

The Ghost of Banquo enters, and sits in Macbeth's place.

Macb. Here had we now our country's honour roof'd,   40
  Were the graced person of our Banquo present;
  Who may I rather challenge for unkindness
  Than pity for mischance!

Ross.   His absence, sir,
  Lays blame upon his promise. Please't your
      highness
  To grace us with your royal company.

Macb. The table's full.

Len.   Here is a place reserved, sir.

Macb. Where?

Len. Here, my good lord. What is't that moves your
      highness?

Macb. Which of you have done this?

Lords.   What, my good lord?

Macb. Thou canst not say I did it: never shake   50
  Thy gory locks at me.

Ross. Gentlemen, rise; his highness is not well.

Lady M Sit, worthy friends: my lord is often thus,
  And hath been from his youth: pray you, keep
      seat;

71

The fit is momentary; upon a thought
He will again be well: if much you note him,
You shall offend him and extend his passion:
Feed, and regard him not. Are you a man?

Macb. Ay, and a bold one, that dare look on that
Which might appal the devil.

Lady M.   O proper stuff!   60
This is the very painting of your fear:
This is the air-drawn dagger which, you said,
Led you to Duncan. O, these flaws and starts,
Impostors to true fear, would well become
A woman's story at a winter's fire,
Authorized by her grandam. Shame itself!
Why do you make such faces? When all's done,
You look but on a stool.

Macb. Prithee, see there! behold! look! lo! how say you?
Why, what care I? If thou canst nod, speak too.   70
If charnel-houses and our graves must send
Those that we bury back, our monuments
Shall be the maws of kites. *Exit Ghost.*

Lady M.   What, quite unmann'd in folly?

Macb. If I stand here, I saw him.

Lady M.   Fie, for shame!

Macb. Blood hath been shed ere now, i' the olden
         time,
Ere humane statute purged the gentle weal;
Ay, and since too, murders have been perform'd
Too terrible for the ear: the time has been,
That, when the brains were out, the man would
         die,
And there an end; but now they rise again,   80
With twenty mortal murders on their crowns,
And push us from our stools: this is more strange
Than such a murder is.

Lady M.   My worthy lord,
Your noble friends do lack you.

Macb.   I do forget.
    Do not muse at me, my most worthy friends;
    I have a strange infirmity, which is nothing
    To those that know me. Come, love and health
        to all;
    Then I'll sit down. Give me some wine, fill full.
    I drink to the general joy o' the whole table,
    And to our dear friend Banquo, whom we miss;   90
    Would he were here! to all and him we thirst,
    And all to all.

Lords.   Our duties, and the pledge.

Re-enter Ghost.

Macb. Avaunt! and quit my sight! let the earth hide
        thee!
    Thy bones are marrowless, thy blood is cold;
    Thou hast no speculation in those eyes
    Which thou dost glare with.

Lady M.   Think of this, good peers,
    But as a thing of custom: 'tis no other;
    Only it spoils the pleasure of the time.

Macb. What man dare, I dare:
    Approach thou like the rugged Russian bear,   100
    The arm'd rhinoceros, or the Hyrcan tiger;
    Take any shape but that, and my firm nerves
    Shall never tremble: or be alive again,
    And dare me to the desert with thy sword;
    If trembling I inhabit then, protest me
    The baby of a girl. Hence, horrible shadow!
    Unreal mockery, hence! [*Exit Ghost.*]
                          Why, so: being gone,
    I am a man again. Pray you, sit still.

Lady M. You have displaced the mirth, broke the good
        meeting,
    With most admired disorder.

Macb.   Can such things be,   110
    And overcome us like a summer's cloud,

Without our special wonder? You make me
    strange
Even to the disposition that I owe,
When now I think you can behold such sights,
And keep the natural ruby of your cheeks,
When mine is blanch'd with fear.

Ross.   What sights, my lord?

Lady M. I pray you, speak not; he grows worse and worse;
    Question enrages him: at once, good night:
    Stand not upon the order of your going,
    But go at once.

Len.   Good night; and better health 120
    Attend his majesty!

Lady M.   A kind good night to all!

Exeunt all but Macbeth and Lady M.

Macb. It will have blood: they say blood will have
    blood:
    Stones have been known to move and trees to
    speak;
    Augures and understood relations have
    By maggot-pies and choughs and rooks
    brought forth
    The secret'st man of blood. What is the night?

Lady M. Almost at odds with morning, which is which.

Macb. How say'st thou, that Macduff denies his person
    At our great bidding?

Lady M.   Did you send to him, sir?

Macb. I hear it by the way, but I will send: 130
    There's not a one of them but in his house
    I keep a servant fee'd. I will to-morrow,
    And betimes I will, to the weird sisters:
    More shall they speak, for now I am bent to
    know,
    By the worst means, the worst. For mine own
    good

All causes shall give way: I am in blood
Stepp'd in so far that, should I wade no more,
Returning were as tedious as go o'er:
Strange things I have in head that will to hand,
Which must be acted ere they may be scann'd. 140

Lady M. You lack the season of all natures, sleep.

Macb. Come, we'll to sleep. My strange and self-abuse
Is the initiate fear that wants hard use:
We are yet but young in deed.

Exeunt.

SCENE V

A heath.

Thunder. Enter the three Witches, meeting Hecate.

First Witch. Why, how now, Hecate! you look angerly.

Hec. Have I not reason, beldams as you are,
Saucy and over-bold? How did you dare
To trade and traffic with Macbeth
In riddles and affairs of death;
And I, the mistress of your charms,
The close contriver of all harms,
Was never call'd to bear my part,
Or show the glory of our art?
And, which is worse, all you have done 10
Hath been but for a wayward son,
Spiteful and wrathful; who, as others do,
Loves for his own ends, not for you.
But make amends now: get you gone,
And at the pit of Acheron
Meet me i' the morning: thither he
Will come to know his destiny:
Your vessels and your spells provide,
Your charms and every thing beside.

I am for the air; this night I'll spend   20
Unto a dismal and a fatal end:
Great business must be wrought ere noon:
Upon the corner of the moon
There hangs a vaporous drop profound;
I'll catch it ere it come to ground:
And that distill'd by magic sleights
Shall raise such artificial sprites
As by the strength of their illusion
Shall draw him on to his confusion:
He shall spurn fate, scorn death, and bear   30
His hopes 'bove wisdom, grace and fear:
And you all know security
Is mortals' chiefest enemy.

Music and a song within: 'Come away, come away,' &c.

Hark! I am call'd; my little spirit, see,
Sits in a foggy cloud, and stays for me. *Exit.*

First Witch. Come, let's make haste; she'll soon be back again.

Exeunt.

SCENE VI

Forres. The palace.

Enter Lennox and another Lord.

Len. My former speeches have but hit your thoughts,
Which can interpret farther: only I say
Things have been strangely borne. The gracious
    Duncan
Was pitied of Macbeth: marry, he was dead:
And the right-valiant Banquo walk'd too late;
Whom, you may say, if't please you, Fleance kill'd
For Fleance fled: men must not walk too late.
Who cannot want the thought, how monstrous
It was for Malcolm and for Donalbain

To kill their gracious father? damned fact!   10
How it did grieve Macbeth! did he not straight,
In pious rage, the two delinquents tear,
That were the slaves of drink and thralls of sleep?
Was not that nobly done? Ay, and wisely too;
For 'twould have anger'd any heart alive
To hear the men deny't. So that, I say,
He has borne all things well: and I do think
That, had he Duncan's sons under his key—
As, an't please heaven, he shall not—they
    should find
What 'twere to kill a father; so should Fleance.   20
But, peace! for from broad words, and 'cause
    he fail'd
His presence at the tyrant's feast, I hear,
Macduff lives in disgrace: sir, can you tell
Where he bestows himself?

Lord.   The son of Duncan,
From whom this tyrant holds the due of birth,
Lives in the English court, and is received
Of the most pious Edward with such grace
That the malevolence of fortune nothing
Takes from his high respect. Thither Macduff
Is gone to pray the holy king, upon his aid   30
To wake Northumberland and warlike Siward:
That by the help of these, with Him above
To ratify the work, we may again
Give to our tables meat, sleep to our nights,
Free from our feasts and banquets bloody knives,
Do faithful homage and receive free honours:
All which we pine for now: and this report
Hath so exasperate the king that he
Prepares for some attempt of war.

Len.   Sent he to Macduff?

Lord. He did: and with an absolute 'Sir, not I,'   40
The cloudy messenger turns me his back,
And hums, as who should say 'You'll rue the time
That clogs me with this answer.'

Len.   And that well might
          Advise him to a caution, to hold what distance
          His wisdom can provide. Some holy angel
          Fly to the court of England and unfold
          His message ere he come, that a swift blessing
          May soon return to this our suffering country
          Under a hand accursed!

Lord.   I'll send my prayers with him.

Exeunt.

ACT FOURTH
SCENE I

A cavern. In the middle, a boiling cauldron.

Thunder. Enter the three Witches.

First Witch. Thrice the brinded cat hath mew'd.

Sec.Witch. Thrice and once the hedge-pig whined.

Third Witch. Harpier cries ''Tis time, 'tis time.'

First Witch. Round about the cauldron go:
          In the poison'd entrails throw.
          Toad, that under cold stone
          Days and nights has thirty one
          Swelter'd venom sleeping got,
          Boil thou first i' the charmed pot.

All.   Double, double toil and trouble;   10
          Fire burn and cauldron bubble.

Sec.Witch. Fillet of a fenny snake,
          In the cauldron boil and bake;
          Eye of newt and toe of frog,
          Wool of bat and tongue of dog,
          Adder's fork and blind-worm's sting,
          Lizard's leg and howlet's wing,

> For a charm of powerful trouble,
> Like a hell-broth boil and bubble.

All. Double, double toil and trouble;   20
      Fire burn and cauldron bubble.

Third Witch. Scale of dragon, tooth of wolf,
      Witches' mummy, maw and gulf
      Of the ravin'd salt-sea shark,
      Root of hemlock digg'd i' the dark,
      Liver of blaspheming Jew,
      Gall of goat and slips of yew
      Sliver'd in the moon's eclipse,
      Nose of Turk and Tartar's lips,
      Finger of birth-strangled babe   30
      Ditch-deliver'd by a drab,
      Make the gruel thick and slab:
      Add thereto a tiger's chaudron,
      For the ingredients of our cauldron.

All. Double, double toil and trouble;
      Fire burn and cauldron bubble.

Sec.Witch. Cool it with a baboon's blood,
      Then the charm is firm and good.

Enter Hecate to the other three Witches.

Hec. O, well done! I commend your pains;
      And every one shall share i' the gains: 40
      And now about the cauldron sing,

      Like elves and fairies in a ring,
      Enchanting all that you put in.

Music and a song: 'Black spirits,' &c.

Hecate retires.

Sec.Witch. By the pricking of my thumbs,
      Something wicked this way comes:
      Open, locks,
      Whoever knocks!

Enter Macbeth.

Macb. How now, you secret, black, and midnight hags!
    What is't you do?

All.   A deed without a name.

Macb. I conjure you, by that which you profess,   50
    Howe'er you come to know it, answer me:
    Though you untie the winds and let them fight
    Against the churches; though the yesty waves
    Confound and swallow navigation up;
    Though bladed corn be lodged and trees blown
        down;
    Though castles topple on their warders' heads;
    Though palaces and pyramids do slope
    Their heads to their foundations; though the
        treasure
    Of nature's germins tumble all together,
    Even till destruction sicken; answer me   60
    To what I ask you.

First Witch.   Speak.

Sec. Witch.   Demand.

Third Witch.   We'll answer.

First Witch. Say, if thou'dst rather hear it from our mouths,
    Or from our masters?

Macb.   Call 'em, let me see 'em.

First Witch. Pour in sow's blood, that hath eaten
    Her nine farrow; grease that's sweaten
    From the murderer's gibbet throw
    Into the flame.

All.   Come, high or low;
    Thyself and office deftly show!

Thunder. First Apparition: an armed Head.

Macb. Tell me, thou unknown power,—

First Witch.   He knows thy thought:
    Hear his speech, but say thou nought.   70

First App. Macbeth! Macbeth! Macbeth! Beware Macduff;
    Beware the thane of Fife. Dismiss me: enough.

Descends.

  Macb. Whate'er thou art, for thy good caution thanks;
    Thou hast harp'd my fear aright: but one word
    more,—

First Witch. He will not be commanded: here's another,
    More potent than the first.

Thunder. Second Apparition: a bloody Child.

  Sec.App. Macbeth! Macbeth! Macbeth!

  Macb. Had I three ears, I'ld hear thee.

  Sec.App. Be bloody, bold and resolute; laugh to scorn
    The power of man, for none of woman born   80
    Shall harm Macbeth. *Descends.*

  Macb. Then live, Macduff: what need I fear of thee?
    But yet I'll make assurance doubly sure,
    And take a bond of fate: thou shalt not live;
    That I may tell pale-hearted fear it lies,
    And sleep in spite of thunder.

Thunder. Third Apparition: a Child crowned, with a tree in his hand.

                          What is this,
    That rises like the issue of a king,
    And wears upon his baby-brow the round
    And top of sovereignty?

  All.   Listen, but speak not to't.

  Third App. Be lion-mettled, proud, and take no care   90
    Who chafes, who frets, or where conspirers are:
    Macbeth shall never vanquish'd be until
    Great Birnam wood to high Dunsinane hill
    Shall come against him. *Descends.*

  Macb.   That will never be:
    Who can impress the forest, bid the tree
    Unfix his earth-bound root? Sweet bodements! good!

Rebellion's head, rise never, till the wood
Of Birnam rise, and our high-placed Macbeth
Shall live the lease of nature, pay his breath
To time and mortal custom. Yet my heart   100
Throbs to know one thing: tell me, if your art
Can tell so much: shall Banquo's issue ever
Reign in this kingdom?

All.   Seek to know no more.

Macb. I will be satisfied: deny me this,
And an eternal curse fall on you! Let me know:
Why sinks that cauldron? and what noise is
    this?

Hautboys.

First Witch. Show!

Sec.Witch. Show!

Third Witch. Show!

All.   Show his eyes, and grieve his heart;   110
Come like shadows, so depart!

*A show of eight Kings, the last with a glass in his hand; Banquo's
Ghost following.*

Macb. Thou art too like the spirit of Banquo: down!
Thy crown does sear mine eye-balls. And thy hair,
Thou other gold-bound brow, is like the first.
A third is like the former. Filthy hags!
Why do you show me this? A fourth! Start, eyes!
What, will the line stretch out to the crack of
    doom?
Another yet! A seventh! I'll see no more:
And yet the eighth appears, who bears a glass
Which shows me many more; and some I see   120
That two-fold balls and treble sceptres carry:
Horrible sight! Now I see 'tis true;
For the blood-bolter'd Banquo smiles upon me,
And points at them for his. What, is this so?

First Witch. Ay, sir, all this is so: but why
    Stands Macbeth thus amazedly?
    Come, sisters, cheer we up his sprites,
    And show the best of our delights:
    I'll charm the air to give a sound,
    While you perform your antic round,   130
    That this great king may kindly say
    Our duties did his welcome pay.

Music. The Witches dance, and then vanish, with Hecate.

Macb. Where are they? Gone? Let this pernicious hour
    Stand aye accursed in the calendar!
    Come in, without there!

Enter Lennox.

Len.   What's your grace's will?

Macb. Saw you the weird sisters?

Len.   No, my lord.

Macb. Came they not by you?

Len.   No indeed, my lord.

Macb. Infected be the air whereon they ride,
    And damn'd all those that trust them! I did hear
    The galloping of horse: who was't came by?   140

Len. 'Tis two or three, my lord, that bring you word
    Macduff is fled to England.

Macb.   Fled to England!

Len. Ay, my good lord.

Macb. [*Aside*] Time, thou anticipatest my dread exploits:
    The flighty purpose never is o'ertook
    Unless the deed go with it: from this moment
    The very firstlings of my heart shall be
    The firstlings of my hand. And even now,
    To crown my thoughts with acts, be it thought
      and done:
    The castle of Macduff I will surprise;   150

Seize upon Fife; give to the edge o' the sword
His wife, his babes, and all unfortunate souls
That trace him in his line. No boasting like a
    fool;
This deed I'll do before this purpose cool:
But no more sights!—Where are these
    gentlemen?
Come, bring me where they are.

Exeunt.

SCENE II

Fife. Macduff's castle.

Enter Lady Macduff, her Son, and Ross.

L. Macd. What had he done, to make him fly the land?

Ross. You must have patience, madam.

L. Macd.   He had none:
    His flight was madness: when our actions do not,
    Our fears do make us traitors.

Ross.   You know not
    Whether it was his wisdom or his fear.

L. Macd. Wisdom! to leave his wife, to leave his babes,
    His mansion and his titles, in a place
    From whence himself does fly? He loves us not;
    He wants the natural touch: for the poor wren,
    The most diminutive of birds, will fight,   10
    Her young ones in her nest, against the owl.
    All is the fear and nothing is the love;
    As little is the wisdom, where the flight
    So runs against all reason.

Ross.   My dearest coz,
    I pray you, school yourself: but, for your husband,
    He is noble, wise, judicious, and best knows

84

The fits o' the season. I dare not speak much
    further:
But cruel are the times, when we are traitors
And do not know ourselves; when we hold
    rumour
From what we fear, yet know not what we fear,   20
But float upon a wild and violent sea
Each way and move. I take my leave of you:
Shall not be long but I'll be here again:
Things at the worst will cease, or else climb
    upward
To what they were before. My pretty cousin,
Blessing upon you!

L. Macd. Father'd he is, and yet he's fatherless.

Ross. I am so much a fool, should I stay longer,
    It would be my disgrace and your discomfort:
    I take my leave at once. *Exit.*

L. Macd.   Sirrah, your father's dead: 30
    And what will you do now? How will you live?

Son. As birds do, mother.

L. Macd.   What, with worms and flies?

Son. With what I get, I mean; and so do they.

L. Macd. Poor bird! thou'ldst never fear the net nor lime,
    The pitfall nor the gin.

Son. Why should I, mother? Poor birds they are not
    set for.
    My father is not dead, for all your saying.

L. Macd. Yes, he is dead: how wilt thou do for a father?

Son. Nay, how will you do for a husband?

L. Macd. Why, I can buy me twenty at any market.   40

Son. Then you'll buy 'em to sell again.

L. Macd. Thou speak'st with all thy wit, and yet, i' faith,
    With wit enough for thee.

Son. Was my father a traitor, mother?

L. Macd. Ay, that he was.

Son. What is a traitor?

L. Macd. Why, one that swears and lies.

Son. And be all traitors that do so?

L. Macd. Every one that does so is a traitor, and must be
           hanged.   50

Son. And must they all be hanged that swear and
           lie?

L. Macd. Every one.

Son. Who must hang them?

L. Macd. Why, the honest men.

Son. Then the liars and swearers are fools; for there
are liars and swearers enow to beat the honest
men and hang up them.

L. Macd. Now, God help thee, poor monkey!
But how wilt thou do for a father?   60

Son. If he were dead, you'ld weep for him: if you
would not, it were a good sign that I should
quickly have a new father.

L. Macd. Poor prattler, how thou talk'st!

Enter a Messenger.

Mess. Bless you, fair dame! I am not to you known,
Though in your state of honour I am perfect.
I doubt some danger does approach you nearly:
If you will take a homely man's advice,
Be not found here; hence, with your little ones.
To fright you thus, methinks I am too savage;   70
To do worse to you were fell cruelty,
Which is too nigh your person. Heaven
      preserve you!
I dare abide no longer. *Exit.*

L. Macd.   Whither should I fly?
        I have done no harm. But I remember now
        I am in this earthly world, where to do harm
        Is often laudable, to do good sometime
        Accounted dangerous folly: why then, alas,
        Do I put up that womanly defence,
        To say I have done no harm?—What are these
                faces?

Enter Murderers.

First Mur. Where is your husband?   80

L. Macd. I hope, in no place so unsanctified
        Where such as thou mayst find him.

First Mur.   He's a traitor.

Son.   Thou liest, thou shag-ear'd villain!

First Mur.   What, you egg!

Stabbing him.

        Young fry of treachery!

Son.   He has kill'd me, mother:
        Run away, I pray you! *Dies.*

                Exit Lady Macduff, crying 'Murderer!'

                Exeunt murderers, following her.

SCENE III

⟨longdash⟩▶◀⟨longdash⟩

England. Before the King's palace.

Enter Malcolm and Macduff.

Mal.   Let us seek out some desolate shade, and there
        Weep our sad bosoms empty.

Macd.   Let us rather

Hold fast the mortal sword, and like good men
Bestride our down-fall'n birthdom: each new morn
New widows howl, new orphans cry, new sorrows
Strike heaven on the face, that it resounds
As if it felt with Scotland and yell'd out
Like syllable of dolour.

Mal.   What I believe, I'll wail;
What know, believe; and what I can redress,
As I shall find the time to friend, I will.   10
What you have spoke, it may be so perchance.
This tyrant, whose sole name blisters our tongues,
Was once thought honest: you have loved him
    well;
He hath not touch'd you yet. I am young; but
    something
You may deserve of him through me; and
    wisdom
To offer up a weak, poor, innocent lamb
To appease an angry god.

Macd. I am not treacherous.

Mal.   But Macbeth is.
A good and virtuous nature may recoil
In an imperial charge. But I shall crave your
    pardon;   20
That which you are, my thoughts cannot
    transpose:
Angels are bright still, though the brightest fell:
Though all things foul would wear the brows
    of grace,
Yet grace must still look so.

Macd.   I have lost my hopes.

Mal. Perchance even there where I did find my doubts.
Why in that rawness left you wife and child,
Those precious motives, those strong knots of
    love,
Without leave-taking? I pray you,
Let not my jealousies be your dishonours,

But mine own safeties. You may be rightly just,
Whatever I shall think.

Macd.   Bleed, bleed, poor country: 31
Great tyranny, lay thou thy basis sure,
For goodness dare not check thee: wear thou
    thy wrongs;
The title is affeer'd. Fare thee well, lord:
I would not be the villain that thou think'st
For the whole space that's in the tyrant's grasp
And the rich East to boot.

Mal.   Be not offended:
I speak not as in absolute fear of you.
I think our country sinks beneath the yoke;
It weeps, it bleeds, and each new day a gash   40
Is added to her wounds: I think withal
There would be hands uplifted in my right;
And here from gracious England have I offer
Of goodly thousands: but for all this,
When I shall tread upon the tyrant's head,
Or wear it on my sword, yet my poor country
Shall have more vices than it had before,
More suffer and more sundry ways than ever,
By him that shall succeed.

Macd.   What should he be?

Mal. It is myself I mean: in whom I know   50
All the particulars of vice so grafted
That, when they shall be open'd, black Macbeth
Will seem as pure as snow, and the poor state
Esteem him as a lamb, being compared
With my confineless harms.

Macd.   Not in the legions
Of horrid hell can come a devil more damn'd
In evils to top Macbeth.

Mal.   I grant him bloody,
Luxurious, avaricious, false, deceitful,
Sudden, malicious, smacking of every sin
That has a name: but there's no bottom, none,   60

In my voluptuousness: your wives, your
    daughters,
Your matrons, and your maids, could not fill up
The cistern of my lust, and my desire
All continent impediments would o'erbear,
That did oppose my will: better Macbeth
Than such an one to reign.

Macd.   Boundless intemperance
In nature is a tyranny; it hath been
The untimely emptying of the happy throne,
And fall of many kings. But fear not yet
To take upon you what is yours: you may   70
Convey your pleasures in a spacious plenty,
And yet seem cold, the time you may so
    hoodwink:
We have willing dames enough; there cannot be
That vulture in you, to devour so many
As will to greatness dedicate themselves,
Finding it so inclined.

Mal.   With this there grows
In my most ill-composed affection such
A stanchless avarice that, were I king,
I should cut off the nobles for their lands,
Desire his jewels and this other's house: 80
And my more-having would be as a sauce
To make me hunger more, that I should forge
Quarrels unjust against the good and loyal,
Destroying them for wealth.

Macd.   This avarice
Sticks deeper, grows with more pernicious root
Than summer-seeming lust, and it hath been
The sword of our slain kings: yet do not fear;
Scotland hath foisons to fill up your will
Of your mere own: all these are portable,
With other graces weigh'd.   90

Mal. But I have none: the king-becoming graces,
As justice, verity, temperance, stableness,
Bounty, perseverance, mercy, lowliness,

Devotion, patience, courage, fortitude,
I have no relish of them, but abound
In the division of each several crime,
Acting it many ways. Nay, had I power, I should
Pour the sweet milk of concord into hell,
Uproar the universal peace, confound
All unity on earth.

Macd.   O Scotland, Scotland!   100

Mal.   If such a one be fit to govern, speak:
I am as I have spoken.

Macd.   Fit to govern!
No, not to live. O nation miserable!
With an untitled tyrant bloody-scepter'd,
When shalt thou see thy wholesome days again,
Since that the truest issue of thy throne
By his own interdiction stands accursed,
And does blaspheme his breed? Thy royal father
Was a most sainted king: the queen that bore
    thee,
Oftener upon her knees than on her feet,   110
Died every day she lived. Fare thee well!
These evils thou repeat'st upon thyself
Have banish'd me from Scotland. O my breast,
Thy hope ends here!

Mal.   Macduff, this noble passion,
Child of integrity, hath from my soul
Wiped the black scruples, reconciled my thoughts
To thy good truth and honour. Devilish Macbeth
By many of these trains hath sought to win me
Into his power; and modest wisdom plucks me
From over-credulous haste: but God above   120
Deal between thee and me! for even now
I put myself to thy direction, and
Unspeak mine own detraction; here abjure
The taints and blames I laid upon myself,
For strangers to my nature. I am yet
Unknown to woman, never was forsworn,
Scarcely have coveted what was mine own,

At no time broke my faith, would not betray
The devil to his fellow, and delight
No less in truth than life: my first false speaking   130
Was this upon myself: what I am truly,
Is thine and my poor country's to command:
Whither indeed, before thy here-approach,
Old Siward, with ten thousand warlike men,
Already at a point, was setting forth.
Now we'll together, and the chance of goodness
Be like our warranted quarrel! Why are you
    silent?

Macd. Such welcome and unwelcome things at once
    'Tis hard to reconcile.

Enter a Doctor.

Mal. Well, more anon. Comes the king forth, I pray
    you?   140

Doct. Ay, sir; there are a crew of wretched souls
That stay his cure: their malady convinces
The great assay of art; but at his touch,
Such sanctity hath heaven given his hand,
They presently amend.

Mal.   I thank you, doctor. *Exit Doctor.*

Macd. What's the disease he means?

Mal.   'Tis call'd the evil:
A most miraculous work in this good king;
Which often, since my here-remain in England,
I have seen him do. How he solicits heaven,
Himself best knows: but strangely-visited people,   150
All swoln and ulcerous, pitiful to the eye,
The mere despair of surgery, he cures,
Hanging a golden stamp about their necks,
Put on with holy prayers: and 'tis spoken,
To the succeeding royalty he leaves
The healing benediction. With this strange virtue
He hath a heavenly gift of prophecy,
And sundry blessings hang about his throne
That speak him full of grace.

Enter Ross.

Macd.   See, who comes here?

Mal.   My countryman; but yet I know him not.   160

Macd. My ever gentle cousin, welcome hither.

Mal.   I know him now: good God, betimes remove
         The means that makes us strangers!

Ross.   Sir, amen.

Macd. Stands Scotland where it did?

Ross.   Alas, poor country!
         Almost afraid to know itself! It cannot
         Be call'd our mother, but our grave: where
             nothing,
         But who knows nothing, is once seen to smile;
         Where sighs and groans and shrieks that rend
             the air,
         Are made, not mark'd; where violent sorrow
             seems
         A modern ecstasy: the dead man's knell   170
         Is there scarce ask'd for who; and good men's
             lives
         Expire before the flowers in their caps,
         Dying or ere they sicken.

Macd.   O, relation
         Too nice, and yet too true!

Mal.   What's the newest grief?

Ross. That of an hour's age doth hiss the speaker;
         Each minute teems a new one.

Macd.   How does my wife?

Ross. Why, well.

Macd.   And all my children?

Ross.   Well too.

Macd. The tyrant has not batter'd at their peace?

Ross. No; they were well at peace when I did leave 'em.

Macd. Be not a niggard of your speech: how goes't?   180

Ross. When I came hither to transport the tidings,
Which I have heavily borne, there ran a rumour
Of many worthy fellows that were out;
Which was to my belief witness'd the rather,
For that I saw the tyrant's power a-foot:
Now is the time of help; your eye in Scotland
Would create soldiers, make our women fight,
To doff their dire distresses.

Mal.   Be't their comfort
We are coming thither: gracious England hath
Lent us good Siward and ten thousand men;   190
An older and a better soldier none
That Christendom gives out.

Ross.   Would I could answer
This comfort with the like! But I have words
That would be howl'd out in the desert air,
Where hearing should not latch them.

Macd.   What concern they?
The general cause? or is it a fee-grief
Due to some single breast?

Ross.   No mind that's honest
But in it shares some woe, though the main
    part
Pertains to you alone.

Macd.   If it be mine,
Keep it not from me, quickly let me have it.   200

Ross. Let not your ears despise my tongue for ever,
Which shall possess them with the heaviest sound
That ever yet they heard.

Macd.   Hum! I guess at it.

Ross. Your castle is surprised; your wife and babes
Savagely slaughter'd: to relate the manner,
Were, on the quarry of these murder'd deer,

　　　　To add the death of you.

Mal.　　　　　　　　　　Merciful heaven!
　　　What, man! ne'er pull your hat upon your brows;
　　　Give sorrow words: the grief that does not speak
　　　Whispers the o'erfraught heart, and bids it break.　　　210

Macd. My children too?

Ross.　　　　　　　　　Wife, children, servants, all　　211
　　　That could be found.

Macd.　　　　　　　　And I must be from thence!
　　　My wife kill'd too?

Ross.　　　I have said.

Mal.　　　　　　Be comforted:
　　　Let's make us medicines of our great revenge,
　　　To cure this deadly grief.

Macd. He has no children. All my pretty ones?
　　　Did you say all? O hell-kite! All?
　　　What, all my pretty chickens and their dam
　　　At one fell swoop?

Mal. Dispute it like a man.

Macd.　　　　　　　　I shall do so;　　　220
　　　But I must also feel it as a man:
　　　I cannot but remember such things were,
　　　That were most precious to me. Did heaven look on,
　　　And would not take their part? Sinful Macduff,
　　　They were all struck for thee! naught that I am,
　　　Not for their own demerits, but for mine,
　　　Fell slaughter on their souls: heaven rest them
　　　　　now!

Mal. Be this the whetstone of your sword: let grief
　　　Convert to anger; blunt not the heart, enrage it.

Macd. O, I could play the woman with mine eyes,　　　230
　　　And braggart with my tongue! But, gentle
　　　　heavens,
　　　Cut short all intermission; front to front

Bring thou this fiend of Scotland and myself;
Within my sword's length set him; if he 'scape,
Heaven forgive him too!

Mal.   This tune goes manly.
Come, go we to the king; our power is ready;
Our lack is nothing but our leave. Macbeth
Is ripe for shaking, and the powers above
Put on their instruments. Receive what cheer
    you may;
The night is long that never finds the day.   240

Exeunt.

ACT FIFTH
SCENE I

━━━━►◆◄━━━━

Dunsinane. Ante-room in the castle.

Enter a Doctor of Physic and a Waiting-Gentlewoman.

Doct. I have two nights watched with you, but can
perceive no truth in your report. When was it
she last walked?

Gent. Since his majesty went into the field, I have
seen her rise from her bed, throw her
nightgown upon her, unlock her closet, take
forth paper, fold it, write upon't, read it,
afterwards seal it, and again return to bed; yet
all this while in a most fast sleep.

Doct. A great perturbation in nature, to receive at   10
once the benefit of sleep and do the effects of
watching! In this slumbery agitation, besides
her walking and other actual performances,
what, at any time, have you heard her say?

Gent. That, sir, which I will not report after her.

Doct. You may to me, and 'tis most meet you should.

Gent. Neither to you nor any one, having no witness   20
to confirm my speech.

Enter Lady Macbeth, with a taper.

Lo you, here she comes! This is her very guise,
and, upon my life, fast asleep. Observe her;
stand close.

Doct. How came she by that light?

Gent. Why, it stood by her: she has light by her
continually; 'tis her command.

Doct. You see, her eyes are open.

Gent. Ay, but their sense is shut.

Doct. What is it she does now? Look, how she rubs   30
her hands.

Gent. It is an accustomed action with her, to seem
thus washing her hands: I have known her
continue in this a quarter of an hour.

Lady M. Yet here's a spot.

Doct. Hark! she speaks: I will set down what comes
from her, to satisfy my remembrance the more
strongly.

Lady M. Out, damned spot! out, I say! One: two: why,
then 'tis time to do't. Hell is murky. Fie, my   40
lord, fie! a soldier, and afeard? What need we
fear who knows it, when none can call our
power to account? Yet who would have thought
the old man to have had so much blood in him?

Doct. Do you mark that?

Lady M. The thane of Fife had a wife; where is she
now? What, will these hands ne'er be clean? No
more o' that, my lord, no more o' that: you
mar all with this starting.   50

Doct. Go to, go to; you have known what you should
not.

Gent. She has spoke what she should not, I am sure
of that: heaven knows what she has known.

Lady M. Here's the smell of the blood still: all the
perfumes of Arabia will not sweeten this little
hand. Oh, oh, oh!

Doct. What a sigh is there! The heart is sorely charged. 60

Gent. I would not have such a heart in my bosom
for the dignity of the whole body.

Doct. Well, well, well,—

Gent. Pray God it be, sir.

Doct. This disease is beyond my practice: yet I have
known those which have walked in their sleep
who have died holily in their beds.

Lady M. Wash your hands; put on your night-gown;
look not so pale: I tell you yet again, Banquo's
buried; he cannot come out on's grave. 70

Doct. Even so?

Lady M. To bed, to bed; there's knocking at the gate:
come, come, come, come, give me your hand:
what's done cannot be undone: to bed, to bed,
to bed. *Exit.*

Doct. Will she go now to bed?

Gent. Directly.

Doct. Foul whisperings are abroad: unnatural deeds
Do breed unnatural troubles: infected minds 80
To their deaf pillows will discharge their
secrets:
More needs she the divine than the physician.
God, God forgive us all! Look after her;
Remove from her the means of all annoyance,
And still keep eyes upon her. So good night:
My mind she has mated and amazed my sight:
I think, but dare not speak.

Gent.   Good night, good doctor.

                              Exeunt.

SCENE II

━━━━◈◈◈━━━━

The country near Dunsinane.

Drum and colours. Enter Menteith, Caithness, Angus, Lennox, and Soldiers.

Ment. The English power is near, led on by Malcolm,
His uncle Siward and the good Macduff:
Revenges burn in them; for their dear causes
Would to the bleeding and the grim alarm
Excite the mortified man.

Ang.   Near Birnam wood
Shall we well meet them; that way are they
    coming.

Caith. Who knows if Donalbain be with his brother?

Len. For certain, sir, he is not: I have a file
Of all the gentry: there is Siward's son,
And many unrough youths, that even now   10
Protest their first of manhood.

Ment.   What does the tyrant?

Caith. Great Dunsinane he strongly fortifies:
Some say he's mad; others, that lesser hate him,
Do call it valiant fury: but, for certain,
He cannot buckle his distemper'd cause
Within the belt of rule.

Ang.   Now does he feel
His secret murders sticking on his hands;
Now minutely revolts upbraid his faith-breach;
Those he commands move only in command,
Nothing in love: now does he feel his title   20
Hang loose about him, like a giant's robe

99

Upon a dwarfish thief.

Ment. Who then shall blame
His pester'd senses to recoil and start,
When all that is within him does condemn
Itself for being there?

Caith. Well, march we on,
To give obedience where 'tis truly owed:
Meet we the medicine of the sickly weal,
And with him pour we, in our country's purge,
Each drop of us.

Len. Or so much as it needs
To dew the sovereign flower and drown the
weeds.
Make we our march towards Birnam.   31

Exeunt, marching.

SCENE III

Dunsinane. A room in the castle.

Enter Macbeth, Doctor, and Attendants.

Macb. Bring me no more reports; let them fly all:
Till Birnam wood remove to Dunsinane
I cannot taint with fear. What's the boy Malcolm?
Was he not born of woman? The spirits that
know
All mortal consequences have pronounced me
thus:
'Fear not, Macbeth; no man that's born of
woman
Shall e'er have power upon thee. Then fly, false
thanes,
And mingle with the English epicures:
The mind I sway by and the heart I bear
Shall never sag with doubt nor shake with fear.   10

Enter a Servant.

> The devil damn thee black, thou cream-faced
> loon!
> Where got'st thou that goose look?

Serv. There is ten thousand—

Macb. Geese, villain?

Serv. Soldiers, sir.

Macb. Go prick thy face and over-red thy fear,
Thou lily-liver'd boy. What soldiers, patch?
Death of thy soul! those linen cheeks of thine
Are counsellors to fear. What soldiers, whey-face?

Serv. The English force, so please you.

Macb. Take thy face hence. [*Exit Servant.*]
                                    Seyton!—I am sick at heart,
When I behold—Seyton, I say!—This push   20
Will cheer me ever, or disseat me now.
I have lived long enough: my way of life
Is fall'n into the sear, the yellow leaf,
And that which should accompany old age,
As honour, love, obedience, troops of friends,
I must not look to have; but, in their stead,
Curses, not loud but deep, mouth-honour, breath,
Which the poor heart would fain deny, and
    dare not.
Seyton!

Enter Seyton.

Sey. What's your gracious pleasure?

Macb.   What news more?   30

Sey. All is confirm'd, my lord, which was reported.

Macb. I'll fight, till from my bones my flesh be hack'd.
Give me my armour.

Sey.   'Tis not needed yet.

Macb. I'll put it on.

Send out moe horses, skirr the country round;
Hang those that talk of fear. Give me mine
   armour.
How does your patient, doctor?

Doct.   Not so sick, my lord,
As she is troubled with thick-coming fancies,
That keep her from her rest.

Macb.   Cure her of that.
Canst thou not minister to a mind diseased,   40
Pluck from the memory a rooted sorrow,
Raze out the written troubles of the brain,
And with some sweet oblivious antidote
Cleanse the stuff'd bosom of that perilous stuff
Which weighs upon the heart?

Doct.   Therein the patient
Must minister to himself.

Macb. Throw physic to the dogs, I'll none of it.
Come, put mine armour on; give me my staff.
Seyton, send out. Doctor, the thanes fly from me.
Come, sir, dispatch. If thou couldst, doctor, cast
The water of my land, find her disease   51
And purge it to a sound and pristine health,
I would applaud thee to the very echo,
That should applaud again. Pull't off, I say.
What rhubarb, senna, or what purgative drug,
Would scour these English hence? Hear'st thou
    of them?

Doct. Ay, my good lord; your royal preparation
Makes us hear something.

Macb.   Bring it after me.
I will not be afraid of death and bane
Till Birnam forest come to Dunsinane.   60

Doct. [*Aside*] Were I from Dunsinane away and clear,
Profit again should hardly draw me here.

Exeunt.

SCENE IV

Country near Birnam wood.

Drum and colours. Enter Malcolm, old Siward and his Son,
Macduff, Menteith, Caithness, Angus, Lennox, Ross, and Soldiers,
marching.

Mal.   Cousins, I hope the days are near at hand
That chambers will be safe.

Ment.   We doubt it nothing.

Siw.   What wood is this before us?

Ment.   The wood of Birnam.

Mal.   Let every soldier hew him down a bough,
And bear't before him: thereby shall we shadow
The numbers of our host, and make discovery
Err in report of us.

Soldiers.   It shall be done.

Siw.   We learn no other but the confident tyrant
Keeps still in Dunsinane, and will endure
Our setting down before't.

Mal.   'Tis his main hope: 10
For where there is advantage to be given,
Both more and less have given him the revolt,
And none serve with him but constrained things
Whose hearts are absent too.

Macd.   Let our just censures
Attend the true event, and put we on
Industrious soldiership.

Siw.   The time approaches,
That will with due decision make us know
What we shall say we have and what we owe.
Thoughts speculative their unsure hopes relate,

But certain issue strokes must arbitrate: 20
Towards which advance the war.

Exeunt, marching.

SCENE V

Dunsinane. Within the castle.

Enter Macbeth, Seyton, and Soldiers, with drum and colours.

Macb. Hang out our banners on the outward walls;
The cry is still 'They come:' our castle's strength
Will laugh a siege to scorn: here let them lie
Till famine and the ague eat them up:
Were they not forced with those that should be
    ours,
We might have met them dareful, beard to beard,
And beat them backward home.

A cry of women within.

                                    What is that noise?

Sey. It is the cry of women, my good *Lord. Exit.*

Macb. I have almost forgot the taste of fears:
The time has been, my senses would have cool'd   10
To hear a night-shriek, and my fell of hair
Would at a dismal treatise rouse and stir
As life were in't: I have supp'd full with horrors;
Direness, familiar to my slaughterous thoughts,
Cannot once start me.

Re-enter Seyton.

                                    Wherefore was that cry?

Sey. The queen, my lord, is dead.

Macb. She should have died hereafter;
There would have been a time for such a word.

To-morrow, and to-morrow, and to-morrow,
Creeps in this petty pace from day to day,   20
To the last syllable of recorded time;
And all our yesterdays have lighted fools
The way to dusty death. Out, out, brief candle!
Life's but a walking shadow, a poor player
That struts and frets his hour upon the stage
And then is heard no more: it is a tale
Told by an idiot, full of sound and fury,
Signifying nothing.

Enter a Messenger.

Thou comest to use thy tongue; thy story quickly.

Mess.   Gracious my lord,   30
I should report that which I say I saw,
But know not how to do it.

Macb.   Well, say, sir.

Mess.   As I did stand my watch upon the hill,
I look'd toward Birnam, and anon, methought,
The wood began to move.

Macb.   Liar and slave!

Mess.   Let me endure your wrath, if't be not so:
Within this three mile may you see it coming;
I say, a moving grove.

Macb.   If thou speak'st false,
Upon the next tree shalt thou hang alive,
Till famine cling thee: if thy speech be sooth,   40
I care not if thou dost for me as much.
I pull in resolution, and begin
To doubt the equivocation of the fiend
That lies like truth: 'Fear not, till Birnam wood
Do come to Dunsinane;' and now a wood
Comes toward Dunsinane. Arm, arm, and out!
If this which he avouches does appear,
There is nor flying hence nor tarrying here.
I 'gin to be a-weary of the sun,   49
And wish the estate o' the world were now undone.

Ring the alarum-bell! Blow, wind! come, wrack!
At least we'll die with harness on our back.

Exeunt.

SCENE VI

Dunsinane. Before the castle.

*Drum and colours. Enter Malcolm, old Siward, Macduff, and their
Army, with boughs.*

Mal. Now near enough; your leavy screens throw
        down,
      And show like those you are. You, worthy
        uncle,
      Shall, with my cousin, your right noble son,
      Lead our first battle: worthy Macduff and we
      Shall take upon's what else remains to do,
      According to our order.

Siw.   Fare you well.
      Do we but find the tyrant's power to-night,
      Let us be beaten, if we cannot fight.

Macd. Make all our trumpets speak; give them all
        breath,
      Those clamorous harbingers of blood and death.   10

Exeunt.

SCENE VII

Another part of the field.

Alarums. Enter Macbeth.

Macb. They have tied me to a stake; I cannot fly,
But bear-like I must fight the course. What's he
That was not born of woman? Such a one
Am I to fear, or none.

Enter young Siward.

Yo.Siw. What is thy name?

Macb.   Thou'lt be afraid to hear it.

Yo.Siw. No; though thou call'st thyself a hotter name
Than any is in hell.

Macb.   My name's Macbeth.

Yo.Siw. The devil himself could not pronounce a title
More hateful to mine ear.

Macb.   No, nor more fearful.

Yo.Siw. Thou liest, abhorred tyrant; with my sword   10
I'll prove the lie thou speak'st.

They fight, and young Siward is slain.

Macb.   Thou wast born of woman.
But swords I smile at, weapons laugh to scorn,
Brandish'd by man that's of a woman born. *Exit.*

Alarums. Enter Macduff.

Macd. That way the noise is. Tyrant, show thy face!
If thou be'st slain and with no stroke of mine,
My wife and children's ghosts will haunt me still.
I cannot strike at wretched kerns, whose arms
Are hired to bear their staves: either thou,
    Macbeth,

  Or else my sword, with an unbatter'd edge,
  I sheathe again undeeded. There thou shouldst
   be;   20
  By this great clatter, one of greatest note
  Seems bruited: let me find him, fortune!
  And more I beg not. *Exit. Alarums.*

Enter Malcolm and old Siward.

Siw. This way, my lord; the castle's gently render'd:
  The tyrant's people on both sides do fight;
  The noble thanes do bravely in the war;
  The day almost itself professes yours,
  And little is to do.

Mal.   We have met with foes
  That strike beside us.

Siw.   Enter, sir, the castle.

     Exeunt. Alarum.

SCENE VIII

═══►◄═══

Another part of the field.

Enter Macbeth.

Macb. Why should I play the Roman fool, and die
  On mine own sword? whiles I see lives, the gashes
  Do better upon them.

Enter Macduff.

Macd.   Turn, hell-hound, turn!

Macb. Of all men else I have avoided thee:
  But get thee back; my soul is too much charged
  With blood of thine already.

Macd.   I have no words:
  My voice is in my sword, thou bloodier villain

Than terms can give thee out! *They fight.*

Macb.   Thou losest labour:
As easy mayst thou the intrenchant air
With thy keen sword impress as make me bleed: 10
Let fall thy blade on vulnerable crests;
I bear a charmed life, which must not yield
To one of woman born.

Macd.   Despair thy charm,
And let the angel whom thou still hast served
Tell thee, Macduff was from his mother's womb
Untimely ripp'd.

Macb. Accursed be that tongue that tells me so,
For it hath cow'd my better part of man!
And be these juggling fiends no more believed,
That palter with us in a double sense;   20
That keep the word of promise to our ear,
And break it to our hope. I'll not fight with thee.

Macd. Then yield thee, coward,
And live to be the show and gaze o' the time:
We'll have thee, as our rarer monsters are,
Painted upon a pole, and underwrit,
'Here may you see the tyrant.'

Macb.   I will not yield,
To kiss the ground before young Malcolm's feet,
And to be baited with the rabble's curse.
Though Birnam wood be come to Dunsinane,   30
And thou opposed, being of no woman born,
Yet I will try the last: before my body
I throw my warlike shield: lay on, Macduff;
And damn'd be him that first cries 'Hold,
    enough!'

Exeunt, fighting. Alarums.

*Retreat. Flourish. Enter, with drum and colours, Malcolm, old Siward,
Ross, the other Thanes, and Soldiers.*

Mal. I would the friends we miss were safe arrived.

Siw. Some must go off: and yet, by these I see,
So great a day as this is cheaply bought.

Mal. Macduff is missing, and your noble son.

Ross. Your son, my lord, has paid a soldier's debt:
He only lived but till he was a man;   40
The which no sooner had his prowess confirm'd
In the unshrinking station where he fought,
But like a man he died.

Siw.   Then he is dead?

Ross. Ay, and brought off the field: your cause of
         sorrow
Must not be measured by his worth, for then
It hath no end.

Siw.   Had he his hurts before?

Ross. Ay, on the front.

Siw.   Why then, God's soldier be he!
Had I as many sons as I have hairs,
I would not wish them to a fairer death:
And so his knell is knoll'd.

Mal.   He's worth more sorrow,   50
And that I'll spend for him.

Siw.   He's worth no more:
They say he parted well and paid his score:
And so God be with him! Here comes newer
         comfort.

Re-enter Macduff, with Macbeth's head.

Macd. Hail, king! for so thou art: behold, where
         stands
The usurper's cursed head: the time is free:
I see thee compass'd with thy kingdom's pearl,
That speak my salutation in their minds;
Whose voices I desire aloud with mine:
Hail, King of Scotland!

All.   Hail, King of Scotland!

Flourish.

Mal.   We shall not spend a large expense of time   60
Before we reckon with your several loves,
And make us even with you. My thanes and
    kinsmen,
Henceforth be earls, the first that ever Scotland
In such an honour named. What's more to do,
Which would be planted newly with the time,
As calling home our exiled friends abroad
That fled the snares of watchful tyranny,
Producing forth the cruel ministers
Of this dead butcher and his fiend-like queen,
Who, as 'tis thought, by self and violent hands   70
Took off her life; this, and what needful else
That calls upon us, by the grace of Grace
We will perform in measure, time and place:
So thanks to all at once and to each one,
Whom we invite to see us crown'd at Scone.

Flourish. Exeunt.

Glossary

A ONE, a man; (Theobald from Davenant, *'a Thane'*; Grant White, *'a man'*); III. iv. 131.

ABSOLUTE, positive; III. vi. 40.

ABUSE, deceive; II. i. 50.

ACHERON, the river of the infernal regions; III. v. 15.

ADDER'S FORK, the forked tongue of the adder; IV. i. 16.

ADDITION, title; I. iii. 106.

ADDRESS'D THEM, prepared themselves; II. ii. 24.

ADHERE, were in accordance; I. vii. 52.

ADMIRED, wondrous-strange; III. iv. 110.

ADVISE, instruct; III. i. 129.

AFEARD, afraid; I. iii. 96.

AFFECTION, disposition; IV. iii. 77.

AFFEER'D, confirmed; IV. iii. 34.

ALARM, call to arms; V. ii. 4.

ALARUM'D, alarmed; II. i. 53.

ALL, any; III. ii. 11.

———; 'and all to all,' *i.e.* and we all (drink) to all; III. iv. 92.

ALL-THING, in every way; III. i. 13.

A-MAKING, in course of progress; III. iv. 34.

ANGEL, genius, demon; V. viii. 14.

ANGERLY, angrily; III. v. 1.

ANNOYANCE, hurt, harm; V. i. 84.

ANON, immediately; I. i. 10.

ANON, ANON, 'coming, coming'; the general answer of waiters; II. iii. 23.

AN'T, if it; (Ff., *'and't'*); III. vi. 19.

ANTIC, grotesque, old-fashioned; IV. i. 130.

ANTICIPATEST, dost prevent; IV. i. 144.

APACE, quickly; III. iii. 6.

APPLY, be devoted; III. ii. 30.

APPROVE, prove; I. vi. 4.

ARGUMENT, subject, theme; II. iii. 126.

ARM'D, encased in armour; III. iv. 101.

AROINT THEE, begone; I. iii. 6.

ARTIFICIAL, made by art; III. v. 27.

AGUE, fever; V. v. 4 As, as if; II. iv. 18.

ASSAY, 'the great a. of art,' the greatest effort of skill; IV. iii. 143.

ATTEND, await; III. ii. 3.

AUGURES, auguries; (?) augurs; III. iv. 124.

AUTHORIZED BY, given on the authority of; III. iv. 66.

AVOUCH, assert; III. i. 120.

BABY OF A GIRL, (?) girl's doll; according to others, 'feeble child of an immature mother'; III. iv. 106.

BADGED, smeared, marked (as with a badge); II. iii. 107.

BANE, evil, harm; V. iii. 59.

BANK AND SHOAL, sandbank and shallows; I. vii. 6 BATTLE, division of an army; V. vi. 4.

BEGUILE, deceive; I. v. 64.

BELLONA, the goddess of war; I. ii. 54.

BEND UP, strain; I. vii. 79.

BENISON, blessing; II. iv. 40.

BENT, determined; III. iv. 134.

BEST, good, suitable; III. iv. 5.

BESTOW'D, staying; III. i. 30.

BESTOWS HIMSELF, has settled; III. vi. 24.

BESTRIDE, stand over in posture of defence; IV. iii. 4.

BIDES, lies; III. iv. 26.

BILL, catalogue; III. i. 100.

BIRNAM, a high hill twelve miles from Dunsinane; IV. i. 93.

BIRTHDOM, land of our birth, mother-country; IV. iii. 4.

BLADED; 'b. corn,' corn in the blade, when the ear is still green; IV. i. 55.

BLIND-WORM, glow-worm; IV. i. 16.

BLOOD-BOLTER'D, locks matted into hard clotted blood; IV. i. 123.

BLOW, blow upon; I. iii. 15.

BODEMENTS, forebodings; IV. i. 96.

BOOT, 'to b.', in addition; IV. iii. 37.

BORNE, conducted, managed; III. vi. 3.

BORNE IN HAND, kept up by false hopes; III. i. 81.

BOSOM, close and intimate; I. ii. 64.

BRAINSICKLY, madly; II. ii. 46.

BREAK, disclose; I. vii. 48.

BREECH'D, 'having the very hilt, or breech, covered with blood';

(according to some 'covered as with breeches'); II. iii. 122.
BREED, family, parentage; IV. iii. 108.
BRINDED, brindled, streaked; IV. i. 1.
BRING, conduct; II. iii. 52.
BROAD, plain-spoken; III. vi. 21.
BROIL, battle; I. ii. 6.
BROKE OPE, broken open; II. iii. 72.
BUT, only; I. vii. 6.
BY, past; IV. i. 137.
BY THE WAY, casually; III. iv. 130.

CABIN'D, confined; III. iv. 24.
CAPTAINS, trisyllabic; (S. Walker conj. *'captains twain'*); I. ii. 34.
CARELESS, uncared for; I. iv. 11.
CASING, encompassing, all surrounding; III. iv. 23.
'CAUSE, because; III. vi. 21.
CENSURES, opinion; V. iv. 14.
CHAMPION ME, fight in single combat with me; III. i. 72.
CHANCED, happened, taken place; I. iii. 153.
CHAPS, jaws, mouth; I. ii. 22.
CHARGE; 'in an imperial c.', in executing a royal command; IV. iii. 30.
CHARGED, burdened, oppressed; V. i. 60.
CHARNEL-HOUSES, tombs; III. iv. 71
CHAUDRON, entrails; IV. i. 33.
CHILDREN (trisyllabic); IV. iii. 177.
CHOKE THEIR ART, render their skill useless; I. ii. 9.
CHOPPY, chapped; I. iii. 44
CHUCK, a term of endearment; III. ii 45.
CLEAR, serenely; I. v. 72.
——, innocent, guiltless; I. vii. 18.
——, unstained; II. i. 28.
CLEARNESS, clear from suspicion; III. i. 133.
CLEPT, called; III. i. 94.
CLING, shrivel up; V. v. 40.
CLOGS, burdens; III. vi. 43 CLOSE, join, unite; III. ii. 14.
CLOSE, secret; III. v. 7.
CLOSED, enclosed; III. i. 99.
CLOUDY, sullen, frowning; III. vi 41.
COCK, cock-crow; 'the second c.', *i.e.*, about three o'clock in the morning; II. iii. 27.

COIGN OF VANTAGE, convenient corner; I. vi. 7.

COLD, (?) dissyllabic; IV. i. 6.

COLME-KILL, *i.e.* Icolmkill, the cell of St. Columba; II. iv. 33.

COME, which have come; I. iii. 144.

COMMAND UPON, put your commands upon; III. i. 16.

COMMENDATIONS, praises; I. iv. 55

COMMENDS, commits, offers; I. vii. 11.

COMMISSION; 'those in c.', those entrusted with the commission; I iv. 2.

COMPOSITION, terms of peace; I. ii 59.

COMPT; 'in c.', in account; I. vi. 26.

COMPUNCTIOUS, pricking the conscience; I. v. 46.

CONCLUDED, decided; III. i. 141.

CONFINELESS, boundless, limitless; IV. iii. 55.

CONFOUNDS, destroys, ruins; II. ii. 11.

CONFRONTED, met face to face; I. ii.

CONFUSION, destruction; II. iii. 71.

CONSEQUENCES; *v.* mortal; V. iii. 5.

CONSENT, counsel, proposal; II. i. 25.

CONSTANCY, firmness; II. ii. 68.

CONTEND AGAINST, vie with; I. vi. 16.

CONTENT, satisfaction; III. ii. 5.

CONTINENT, restraining; IV. iii. 64.

CONVERT, change; IV. iii. 229.

CONVEY, 'indulge secretly'; IV. iii. 71.

CONVINCE, overpower; I. vii. 64.

CONVINCES, overpowers; IV. iii. 142.

COPY, (?) copyhold, non-permanent tenure; III. ii. 38.

CORPORAL, corporeal; I. iii. 81.

———; 'each c. agent,' *i.e.* 'each faculty of the body'; I. vii. 80.

COUNSELLORS; 'c. to fear,' fear's counsellors, *i.e.* 'suggest fear'; V. iii. 17.

COUNTENANCE, 'be in keeping with'; II. iii. 85.

COURSED, chased; I. vi. 21

CRACK OF DOOM, burst of sound, thunder, at the day of doom; IV. i. 117.

CRACKS, charges; I. ii. 37.

CROWN, head; IV. i. 113.

DAINTY OF, particular about; II. iii. 150.

DAM, mother; IV. iii. 218

DEAR, deeply felt; V. ii. 3.

DEGREES, degrees of rank; III. iv. 1.

DELIVER THEE, report to thee; I. v. 11.

DELIVERS, communicates to us; III. iii. 2.

DEMI-WOLVES, a cross between dogs and wolves; III. i. 94.

DENIES, refuses; III. iv. 128.

DETRACTION, defamation; 'mine own d.', the evil things I have spoken against myself; IV. iii. 123.

DEVIL (monosyllabic); I. iii. 107.

DEW, bedew; V. ii. 30.

DIRE COMBUSTION, turbulent commotion; II, iii. 63

DISJOINT, fall to pieces; III. ii. 16.

DISPLACED, banished; III. iv. 109.

DISPUTE IT, fight against it; (?) reason upon it (Schmidt); IV. iii. 220.

DISSEAT, unseat; V. iii. 21.

DISTANCE, hostility; III. i. 116.

DOFF, do off, put off; IV. iii. 188.

DOUBT, fear, suspect; IV. ii. 67.

DRENCHED, drowned; I. vii. 68

DRINK; 'my d.,' *i.e.* 'my *posset*'; II. i. 31.

DROWSE, become drowsy; III. ii. 52.

DUDGEON, handle of a dagger; II. i. 46.

DUNNEST, darkest; I. v. 52.

EARNEST, pledge, money paid beforehand; I. iii. 104.

EASY, easily; II. iii. 143.

ECSTASY, any state of being beside one's self, violent emotion; III. ii. 22.

EFFECTS, acts, actions; V. i. 11.

EGG, term of contempt; IV. ii. 83.

EMINENCE, distinction; III. ii. 31.

ENGLAND, the King of England; IV. iii. 43.

ENKINDLE, incite; I. iii. 121.

ENOW, enough; II. iii. 7.

ENTRANCE (trisyllabic); I. v. 40.

EQUIVOCATE TO HEAVEN, get to heaven by equivocation; II. iii. 12.

EQUIVOCATOR (probably alluding to Jesuitical equivocation; Garnet, the superior of the order was on his trial in March, 1606); II. iii. 10.

ESTATE, royal dignity, succession to the crown; I. iv. 37.

ETERNAL JEWEL, immortal soul; III. i. 68.

ETERNE, perpetual; III. ii. 38.

EVIL, king's evil, scrofula; IV. iii. 146.

EXASPERATE, exasperated; III. vi. 38.

EXPECTATION, those guests who are expected; III. iii. 10.

EXPEDITION, haste; II. iii. 116.

EXTEND, prolong; III. iv. 57.

FACT, act, deed; III. vi. 10.

FACULTIES, powers, prerogatives; I. vii. 17.

FAIN, gladly; V. iii. 28.

FANTASTICAL, imaginary; I. iii. 53; I. iii. 139.

FARROW, litter of pigs; IV. i. 65.

FAVOUR, pardon; I. iii. 149.

——, countenance, face; I. v. 73.

FEARS, objects of fear; I. iii. 137.

FEED, 'to f.', feeding; III. iv. 35.

FEE-GRIEF, 'grief that hath a single owner'; IV. iii. 196.

FELL, scalp; V. v. 11.

——, cruel, dire; IV. ii. 71.

FELLOW, equal; II. iii. 68.

FILE, list; V. ii. 8.

——; 'the valued f.', list of qualities; III. i. 95.

FILED, made foul, defiled; III. i. 65.

FIRST; 'at f. and last,' (?) once for all, from the beginning to the end;
   (Johnson conj. *'to f. and next'*); III. iv. 1.

FITS, caprices; IV. ii. 17.

FLAWS, storms of passion; III. iv. 63.

FLIGHTY, fleeting; IV. i. 145.

FLOUT, mock, defy; I. ii. 49.

FLY, fly from me; V. iii. 1.

FOISONS, plenty, rich harvests; IV. iii. 88.

FOLLOWS, attends; I. vi. 11.

FOR, because of; III. i. 121.

——, as for, as regards; IV. ii. 15.

FORBID, cursed, blasted; I. iii. 21.

FORCED, strengthened; V. v. 5.

FORGE, fabricate, invent; IV. iii. 82.

FORSWORN, perjured; IV. iii. 126.

FOUNDED, firmly fixed; III. iv. 22.

FRAME OF THINGS, universe; III. ii. 16.

FRANCHISED, free, unstained; II. i. 28.

FREE, freely; I. iii. 155.

FREE, honourable; III. vi. 36.

FREE, remove, do away; (Steevens conj. *'Fright'* or *'Fray'*; Bailey conj., adopted by Hudson, *'Keep'* Kinnear conj. *'Rid'*); III. vi. 35.

FRENCH HOSE, probably a reference to the narrow, straight hose, in contra-distinction to the round, wide hose; II. iii. 16.

FRIGHT, frighten, terrify; IV. ii. 70.

FROM, differently from; III. i. 100.

——, in consequence of, on account of; III. vi. 21.

FRY, literally a swarm of young fishes; here used as a term of contempt; IV. ii. 84.

FUNCTION, power of action; I. iii. 140.

FURBISH'D, burnished or well-prepared; I. ii. 32.

GALL, bitterness; I. v. 49

GALLOWGLASSES, heavy-armed Irish troops; (F. 1, *'Gallowgrosses'*); I. ii. 13.

GENIUS, spirit of good or ill; III. i. 56.

GENTLE SENSES, senses which are soothed (by the 'gentle' air); (Warburton, *'general sense'*; Johnson conj., adopted by Capell, *'gentle sense'*); I. vi. 3.

GERMINS, germs, seeds; IV. i. 59.

GET, beget; I. iii. 67.

GIN, a trap to catch birds; IV. ii. 35.

'GINS, begins; I. ii. 25.

GIVES OUT, proclaims; IV. iii. 192.

GOD'ILD US, corruption of *'God yield us'*; (Ff., *'God-eyld us'*); I. vi. 13.

GOLGOTHA, *i.e.* 'the place of a skull' (*cp.* Mark xv. 22); I. ii. 40.

GOOD, brave; IV. iii. 3.

GOODNESS; 'the chance of g.', 'the chance of success'; IV. iii. 136.

GOOSE, a tailor's smoothing iron; II. iii. 17.

GOOSE LOOK, white, fearful appearance; V. iii. 12

GOSPELL'D, imbued with Gospel teaching; III. i. 88.

GO TO, GO TO, an exclamation of reproach; V. i. 51.

GOUTS, drops; II. i. 46.

GRACED, gracious, full of graces; III. iv. 41.

GRANDAM, grandmother; III. iv. 66.

GRAVE, weighty; III. i. 22.

GRAYMALKIN, a grey cat (the familiar spirit of the First Witch; '*malkin*' diminutive of 'Mary'); I. i. 9.

GRIPE, grasp; III. i. 62.

GROOMS, servants of any kind; II. ii. 5.

GULF, gullet; IV. i. 23.

HAIL (dissyllabic); I. ii. 5.

HARBINGER, forerunner, an officer of the king's household; I. iv. 45.

HARDLY, with difficulty; V. iii. 62.

HARMS, injuries; 'my h.', injuries inflicted by me; IV. iii. 55.

HARP'D, hit, touched; IV. i. 74.

HARPIER, probably a corruption of *Harpy*; IV. i. 3.

HAVING, possessions; I. iii. 56.

HEAR, talk with; III. iv. 32.

HEART; 'any h.', the heart of any man; III. vi. 15.

HEAVILY, sadly; IV. iii. 182.

HECATE, the goddess of hell; (one of the names of Artemis-Diana, as goddess of the infernal regions); II. i. 52.

HEDGE-PIG, hedge-hog; IV. i. 2.

HERALD, accompany; I. iii. 102

HERMITS, beadsmen; men bound to pray for their benefactors; (F. 1, '*Ermites*'); I. vi. 20.

HIE THEE, hasten; I. v. 26.

HIS, this man's; IV. iii. 80.

HOLDS, withholds; III. vi. 25.

HOLP, helped; I. vi. 23.

HOME, thoroughly, completely; I. iii. 120.

HOMELY, humble; IV. ii. 68.

HOODWINK, blind; IV. iii. 72.

HORSES (monosyllabic); II. iv. 14.

HOUSEKEEPER, watch dog; III. i. 97.

HOWLET'S, owlet's; IV. i. 17.

HOW SAY'ST THOU, what do you think; III. iv. 128.

HUMANE, human; III. iv. 76.

HURLYBURLY, tumult, uproar; I. i. 3.

HUSBANDRY, economy; II. i. 4.

HYRCAN TIGER, *i.e.* tiger of Hyrcania, a district south of the Caspian; III. iv. 101.

IGNORANT, *i.e.* of future events; I. v. 58.

ILL-COMPOSED, compounded of evil qualities; IV. iii. 77.

ILLNESS, evil; I. v. 21.

IMPRESS, force into his service; IV. i. 95.

IN, under the weight of; IV. iii. 20.

INCARNADINE, make red; II. ii. 62.

INFORMS, takes visible form; II. i. 48.

INITIATE; 'the i. fear,' 'the fear that attends, *i.e.* the first initiation (into guilt)'; III. iv. 143.

INSANE; 'the i. root', the root which causes insanity; I. iii. 84.

INSTANT, present moment; I. v. 59.

INTERDICTION, exclusion; IV. iii. 107.

INTERMISSION, delay; IV. iii. 232.

INTRENCHANT, indivisible; V. viii. 9.

JEALOUSIES, suspicions; IV. iii. 29.

JUMP, hazard, risk; I. vii. 7.

JUST, exactly; III. iii. 4.

JUTTY, jetty, projection; I. vi. 6.

KERNS, light-armed Irish troops; I. ii. 13.

KNOWINGS, knowledge, experiences; II. iv. 4.

KNOWLEDGE; 'the k.', what you know; (Collier MS. and Walker conj. '*thy k.*'); I. ii. 6.

LACK, want, requirement; IV. iii. 237.

LACK, miss; III. iv. 84.

LAPP'D, wrapped; I. ii. 54.

LARGE, liberal, unrestrained; III. iv. 11.

LATCH, catch; IV. iii. 195.

LATED, belated; III. iii. 6.

LAVE, keep clear and unsullied; III. ii. 33.

LAVISH, unrestrained, insolent; I. ii. 57.

LAY, did lodge; II. iii. 59.

LEASE OF NATURE, term of natural life; IV. i. 99.

LEAVE, leave off; III. ii. 35.

LEFT UNATTENDED, forsaken, deserted; II. ii. 69.

LESSER, less; V. ii. 13.

LIES; 'swears and l.', *i.e.* 'swears allegiance and commits perjury'; (*cp.* IV. ii. 51 for the literal sense of the phrase); IV. ii. 47.

LIGHTED, descended; II. iii. 148.

LIKE, same; II. i. 30.

——, likely; II. iv. 29.

——, equal, the same; IV. iii. 8.

LILY-LIVER'D, cowardly; V. iii. 15.

LIMBEC, alembic, still; I. vii. 67.

LIME, bird-lime; IV. ii. 34.

LIMITED, appointed; II. iii. 57.

LINE, strengthen; I. iii. 112.

LIST, lists, place marked out for a combat; III. i. 71.

LISTENING, listening to; II. ii. 28.

LO; 'lo you,' *i.e.* look you; V. i. 22.

LODGED, laid, thrown down; IV. i. 55.

LOOK, expect; V. iii. 26.

LOON, brute; V. iii. 11.

LUXURIOUS, lustful; IV. iii. 58.

MAGGOT-PIES, magpies; III. iv. 125.

MALICE DOMESTIC, civil war; III. ii. 25

MANSIONRY, abode; I. vi. 5.

MARK, take heed, listen; I. ii. 28.

——, notice; V. i. 46.

MARRY, a corruption of the Virgin Mary; a slight oath; III. vi. 4.

MATED, bewildered; V. i. 86.

MAWS, stomachs; III. iv. 73.

MAY I, I hope I may; III. iv. 42.

MEDICINE, 'physician'; (?) physic; V. ii. 27.

MEEK, meekly; I. vii. 17.

MEMORIZE, make memorable, make famous; I. ii. 40.

MERE, absolutely; IV. iii. 89.

MERE, utter, absolute; IV. iii. 152.

METAPHYSICAL, supernatural; I. v. 30.

MINION, darling, favourite; I. ii. 19; II. iv. 15.

MINUTELY, 'happening every minute, continual'; V. ii. 18.

MISSIVES, messengers; I. v. 7.

MISTRUST; 'he needs not our m.' *i.e.* we need not mistrust him; III. iii. 2.

MOCKERY, delusive imitation; III. iv. 107.

MODERN, ordinary; IV. iii. 170.

MOE, more; V. iii. 35.

MONSTROUS (trisyllabic); III. vi. 8.

MORTAL, deadly, murderous; I. v. 42.

——, 'm. murders,' deadly wounds; III. iv. 81.

——, 'm. consequences,' what befalls man in the course of time; V. iii. 5.

MORTALITY, mortal life; II. iii. 98.

MORTIFIED, dead, insensible; V. ii. 5

MOUNCH'D, chewed with closed lips; I. iii. 5.

MUSE, wonder; III. iv. 85.

MUST BE, was destined to be; IV. iii. 212.

NAPKINS, handkerchiefs; II. iii. 6.

NATURE; 'nature's mischief,' man's evil propensities; I. v. 51.

——; 'in n.', in their whole nature; II. iv. 16.

NAUGHT, vile thing; IV. iii. 225.

NAVE, navel, middle; (Warburton '*nape*'); I. ii. 22.

NEAR, nearer; II. iii. 146.

NEAR'ST OF LIFE, inmost life, most vital parts; III. i. 118.

NICE, precise, minute; IV. iii. 174.

NIGHTGOWN, dressing gown; II. ii. 70.

NOISE, music; IV. i. 106.

NORWAYS', Norwegians'; I. ii. 59.

NORWEYAN, Norwegian; I. ii. 31.

NOTE, notoriety; III. ii. 44.

——, list; III. iii. 10.

——, notice; III. iv. 56.

NOTHING, not at all; I. iii. 96.

——, nobody; IV. iii. 166.

NOTION, apprehension; III. i. 83.

OBLIVIOUS, causing forgetfulness; V. iii. 43.

OBSCURE; 'o. bird,' *i.e.* the bird delighting in darkness, the owl; II. iii. 64.

ODDS; 'at o.', at variance; III. iv. 127.

O'ERFRAUGHT, overcharged, over-loaded; IV. iii. 210.

OF, from; IV. i. 81.

——, with; (Hanmer, '*with*'); I. ii. 13.

——, over; I. iii. 33.

——, by; III. vi. 4; III. vi. 27.

——, for; IV. iii. 95.

OFFICES, duty, employment; III. iii. 3.

——, *i.e.* domestic offices, servants' quarters; II. i. 14.
OLD (used colloquially); II. iii. 2.
ON, of; I. iii. 84.
ONCE, ever; IV. iii. 167.
ONE, wholly, uniformly; II. ii. 63.
ON'S, of his; V. i. 70.
ON'T, of it; III. i. 114.
OPEN'D, unfolded; IV. iii. 52.
OR ERE, before; IV. iii. 173.
ORNAMAENT OF LIFE, the crown; I. vii. 42
OTHER, others; I. iii. 14.
——, 'the o.', *i.e.* the other side; I. vii. 28.
——, otherwise; I. vii. 77.
OTHER'S, other man's; IV. iii. 80.
OURSELVES, one another; III. iv. 32.
OUT, *i.e.* in the field; IV. iii. 183.
OUTRUN, did outrun; (Johnson, *'outran'*); II. iii. 117.
OVERCOME, overshadow; III. iv. 111.
OVER-RED, redden over; V. iii. 14.
OWE, own, possess; I. iii. 76.
OWED, owned; I. iv. 10.

PADDOCK, toad (the familiar spirit of the second witch); I. i. 10.
PALL, wrap, envelop; I. v. 52.
PARRICIDE, patricide; III. i. 32
PASSION, strong emotion; III. iv. 57.
PATCH, fool (supposed to be derived from the patched or motley coat of
     the jester); V. iii. 15.
PEAK, dwindle away; I. iii. 23.
PENT-HOUSE LID, *i.e.* eye-lids; I. iii. 20.
PERFECT, well, perfectly acquainted; IV. ii. 66.
PESTER'D, troubled; V. ii. 23.
PITFALL, a snare for fowl; IV. ii. 35
PLACE, 'pitch, the highest elevation of a hawk'; a term of falconry; II.
     iv. 12.
POINT; 'at a p.', 'prepared for any emergency'; IV. iii. 135.
POOR, feeble; III. ii. 14.
POORLY, dejectedly, unworthily; II. ii. 72.
PORTABLF, endurable; IV. iii. 89.
POSSESS, fill; IV. iii. 202.

POSSETS, drink; 'posset is hot milk poured on ale or sack, having sugar, grated bisket, and eggs, with other ingredients boiled in it. which goes all to a curd'; (Randle Holmes' *Academy of Armourie*, 1688); II. ii. 6.

POSTERS, speedy travellers; I. iii. 33.

POWER, armed force, army; IV. iii. 185.

PREDOMINANCE, superior power, influence; an astrological term; II. iv. 8.

PRESENT, present time; I. v. 58.

PRESENT, instant, immediate; I. ii. 64.

PRESENT, offer; III. ii. 31.

PRESENTLY, immediately; IV. iii. 145.

PRETENCE, purpose, intention; II. iii. 137.

PRETEND, intend; II. iv. 24.

PROBATION; 'passed in p. with you,' proved, passing them in detail, one by one; III. i. 80.

PROFOUND, 'having deep or hidden qualities' (Johnson); (?) 'deep, and therefore ready to fall' (Clar. Pr.); III. v. 24.

PROOF, proved armour; I. ii. 54.

PROPER, fine, excellent (used ironically); III. iv. 60.

PROTEST, show publicly, proclaim; V. ii. 11.

PURGED, cleansed; III. iv. 76.

PURVEYOR, an officer of the king sent before to provide food for the King and his retinue, as the *harbinger* provided lodging; I. vi. 22.

PUSH, attack, onset; V. iii. 20.

PUT ON, set on, (?) set to work; IV. iii. 239.

PUT UPON, falsely attribute; I. vii. 70.

QUARRY, a heap of slaughtered game; IV. iii. 206.

QUELL, murder; I. vii. 72.

QUIET; 'at q.', in quiet, at peace; II. iii. 18.

RAVELL'D, tangled; II. ii. 37.

RAVIN'D, ravenous; IV. i. 24.

RAVIN UP, devour greedily; II. iv. 28.

RAWNESS, hurry; IV. iii. 26.

READINESS; 'manly r.', complete clothing (opposed to 'naked frailties'); II. iii. 139.

RECEIPT, receptacle; I. vii. 66.

RECEIVED, believed; I. vii. 74.

RECOIL, swerve; IV. iii. 19.

——; 'to r.', for recoiling; V. ii. 23.

REEKING, steaming; I. ii. 39

RELATION, narrative; IV. iii. 173.

RELATIONS, 'the connection of effects with causes'; III. iv. 124.

RELISH, smack; IV. iii. 95.

REMEMBRANCE, quadrisyllabic; III. ii. 30.

REMEMBRANCER, reminder; III. iv. 37.

REMORSE, pity; I. v. 45.

REQUIRE, ask her to give; III. iv. 6.

RESOLVE YOURSELVES, decide, make up your minds; III. i. 138.

REST, remain; I. vi. 20.

——, give rest; IV. iii. 227.

RETURN, give back, render; I. vi. 28.

RONYON, a term of contempt; I. iii. 6.

ROOF'D, gathered under one roof; III. iv. 40.

ROOKY, gloomy, foggy; (Jennens, 'rocky'); III. ii. 51.

ROUND, circlet, crown; I. v. 29.

——; 'r. and top of sovereignty,' *i.e.* 'the crown, the top or summit of sovereign power'; IV. i. 87.

——, dance in a circle; IV. i. 130.

RUBS, hindrances, impediments; III. i. 134.

RUMP-FED, well-fed, pampered; I. iii. 6.

SAFE TOWARD, with a sure regard to; I. iv. 27.

SAG, droop, sink; V. iii. 10.

SAINT COLME'S INCH, the island of Columba, now Inchcolm, in the Firth of Forth; I. ii. 61.

SAUCY, insolent, importunate; (?) pungent, sharp, gnawing (Koppel); III. iv. 25.

SAY TO, tell; I. ii. 6.

'SCAPED, escaped; III. iv. 20.

SCARF UP, blindfold; III. ii. 47.

SCONE, the ancient coronation place of the kings of Scotland; II. iv. 31.

SCOTCH'D, 'cut with shallow incisions' (Theobald's emendation of Ff., 'scorch'd'); III. ii. 13.

SEASON, seasoning; III. iv. 141.

SEAT, situation; I. vi. 1.

SEATED, fixed firmly; I. iii. 136.

SECURITY, confidence, consciousness of security, carelessness; III. v. 32.

SEELING, blinding (originally a term of falconry); III. ii. 46.

SEEMS; 'that s. to speak things strange,' *i.e.* 'whose appearance corresponds with the strangeness of his message' (Clar. Pr.); (Johnson conj. *'teems'*; Collier MS., *'comes,'* etc.); I. ii. 47.

SELF-ABUSE, self-delusion; III. iv. 142.

SELF-COMPARISONS, measuring himself with the other; I. ii. 55.

SELFSAME, very same; I. iii. 88.

SENNET, a set of notes on trumpet or cornet; III. i. 10–11.

SE'NNIGHTS, seven nights, weeks; I. iii. 22.

SENSIBLE, perceptible, tangible; II. i. 36.

SERGEANT (trisyllabic), a captain; I. ii. 3.

SET FORTH, shewed; I. iv. 6.

SETTLED, determined; I. vii. 79.

SEWER, one who tasted each dish to prove there was no poison in it; I. vii. (direct.).

SHADOW, disguise; V. iv. 5

SHAG-EAR'D, having hairy ears; (Steevens conj., adopted by Singer (ed. 2) and Hudson, *'shag-hair'd'*); IV. ii. 83.

SHALL, will; II. i. 29.

——, I shall; IV. ii. 23.

SHAME, am ashamed; II. ii. 64.

SHARD-BORNE, borne by scaly wingcases; (Davenant, *'sharp-brow'd'*; Daniel conj. *'sharn-bode'*; Upton conj. *'sharn-born'*); III. ii. 42.

SHIFT, steal, quietly get; II. iii. 151.

SHIPMAN'S CARD, the card of the compass; I. iii. 17.

SHOUGH, a kind of shaggy dog; (Ff., *'Showghes'*; Capell, *'shocks'*); III. i. 94.

SHOULD BE, appear to be; I. iii. 45.

SHOW, dumb-show; IV. i. 111–112.

SHOW, appear; I. iii. 54.

SHUT UP, enclosed, enveloped; II. i. 16.

SICKEN, be surfeited; IV. i. 60.

SIGHTLESS, invisible; I. vii. 23.

SIGHTS; Collier MS. and Singer MS. *'flights'*; Grant White *'sprites'*; IV. i. 155.

SINEL, Macbeth's father, according to Holinshed; I. iii. 71.

SINGLE, individual; I. iii. 140.

——, simple, small; I. vi. 16.

SIRRAH, used in addressing an inferior; here used playfully; IV. ii. 30.

SKIRR, scour; V. iii. 35.

SLAB, thick, glutinous; IV. i. 32.

SLEAVE, sleave-silk; floss silk; II. ii. 37.

SLEEK O'ER, smooth; III. ii. 27.

SLEIGHTS, feats of dexterity; III. v. 26.

SLIPP'D, let slip; II. iii. 52.

SLIVER'D, slipped off; IV. i. 28.

SMACK, have the taste, savour; I. ii. 44.

So, like grace, gracious; IV. iii. 24.

So WELL, as well; I. ii. 43.

SOLE, alone, mere; IV. iii. 12.

SOLEMN, ceremonious, formal; III. i. 14.

SOLICITING, inciting; I. iii. 130.

SOLICITS, entreats, moves by prayer; IV. iii. 149.

SOMETHING, some distance; III. i. 132.

SOMETIME, sometimes; I. vi. 11.

SORELY, heavily; V. i. 59.

SORRIEST, saddest; III. ii. 9.

SORRY, sad; II. ii. 20.

SPEAK, bespeak, proclaim; IV. iii. 159.

SPECULATION, intelligence; III. iv. 95.

SPEED; 'had the s. of him,' has outstripped him; I. v. 36.

SPONGY, imbibing like a sponge; I. vii. 71.

SPRING, source; I. ii. 27.

SPRITES, spirits; IV. i. 127.

SPY, see Note; III. i. 130.

STABLENESS, constancy; IV. iii. 92.

STAFF, lance; V. iii. 48.

STAMP, stamped coin; IV. iii. 153.

STANCHLESS, insatiable; IV. iii. 78.

STAND, remain; III. i. 4.

STAND NOT UPON, do not be particular about; III. iv. 119.

STATE, chair of State; III. iv. 5.

STATE OF HONOUR, noble rank, condition; IV. ii. 66.

STAVES, clubs; V. vii. 18

STAY, wait for; IV. iii. 142.

STAYS, waits; III. v. 35.

STEEP'D, dyed; II. iii. 121

STICKING-PLACE, i.e. 'the place in which the peg of a stringed
   instrument remains fast; the proper degree of tension'; I. vii. 60.

STIR, stirring, moving; I. iii. 144.

STOREHOUSE, place of burial; II. iv. 34.

STRANGE, new; I. iii. 145.

——; 's. and self-abuse,' *i.e.* (?) 'my abuse of others and myself'; III. iv. 142.

STRANGELY-VISITED, afflicted with strange diseases; IV. iii. 150.

STUFF'D, crammed, full to bursting; V. iii. 44.

SUBORN'D, bribed; II. iv. 24

SUBSTANCES, forms; I. v. 50.

SUDDEN, violent; IV. iii. 59.

SUFFER, perish; III. ii. 16.

SUFFERING; 'our s. country,' *i.e.* our country suffering; III. vi. 48.

SUGGESTION, temptation, incitement; I. iii. 134.

SUMMER-SEEMING, 'appearing like summer; seeming to be the effect of a transitory and short-lived heat of the blood' (Schmidt); (Warburton, '*summer-teeming*'; Johnson, '*fume, or seething,*' &c.); IV. iii, 86.

SUNDRY, various; IV. iii. 48.

SURCEASE, cessation; I. vii. 4.

SURFEITED, drunken; II. ii. 5

SURVEYING, noticing, perceiving; I. ii. 31.

SWAY BY, am directed by; V. iii. 9.

SWEARS, swears allegiance; IV. ii. 47.

TAINT, be infected; V. iii. 3.

TAKING-OFF, murder, death; I. vii. 20.

TEEMS, teems with; IV. iii. 176.

TEMPERANCE, moderation, self-restraint; IV. iii. 92.

TENDING, tendance, attendance; I. v. 38.

TEND ON, wait on; I. v. 42.

THAT, so that; I. ii. 58.

THAT; 'to th.', to that end, for that purpose; I. ii. 10.

THE EVIL, scrofula, a disease in which swollen glands break the skin; IV. iii. 146

THEREWITHAL, therewith; III. i. 34.

THIRST, desire to drink; III. iv. 91.

THOUGHT; 'upon a th.', in as small an interval as one can think a thought; III. iv. 55.

——, being borne in mind; III. i. 132.

THRALLS, slaves, bondmen; III. vi. 13.

THREAT, threaten; II. i. 60.

TILL THAT, till; I. ii. 54.

TIMELY, betimes, early; II. iii. 51.

——, 'to gain the t. inn,' opportune; III. iii. 7.

TITLES, possessions; IV. ii. 7.

To, in addition to; I. vi. 19.

——, according to; III. iii. 4.

——, compared to; III. iv. 64.

——, for, as; IV. iii. 10.

——, linked with, 'prisoner to'; III. iv. 25.

TOP, overtop, surpass; IV. iii. 57.

TOP-FULL, full to the top, brimful; I. v. 43.

TOUCH, affection, feeling; IV. ii. 9.

TOUCH'D, injured, hurt; IV. iii. 14.

TOWERING, turning about, soaring, flying high (a term of falconry); II. iv. 12.

TRACE, follow; IV. i. 153.

TRAINS, artifices, devices; IV. iii. 118.

TRAMMEL UP, entangle as in a net; I. vii. 3.

TRANSPORT, convey; IV. iii. 181.

TRANSPOSE, change; IV. iii. 21.

TREBLE SCEPTRES, symbolical of the three kingdoms—England, Scotland, and Ireland; IV. i. 121.

TRIFLED, made trifling, made to sink into insignificance; II. iv. 4.

TUGG'D; 't. with fortune,' pulled about in wrestling with fortune; III. i. 112.

TWO-FOLD BALLS, probably referring to the double coronation of James, at Scone and Westminster (Clar. Pr.); according to others the reference is to the union of the two islands; IV. i. 121.

TYRANNY, usurpation; IV. iii. 67.

TYRANT, usurper; III. vi. 22.

UNBEND, slacken; II. ii. 45

UNFIX, make to stand on end; I. iii. 135.

UNROUGH, beardless; V. ii. 10.

UNSPEAK, recall, withdraw; IV. iii. 123.

UNTITLED, having no title or claim; IV. iii. 104.

UNTO, to; I. iii. 121.

UPON, to; III. vi. 30.

UPROAR, 'stir up to tumult' (Schmidt); (Ff. 1, 2, 'uprore'; Keightley, 'Uproot'); IV. iii. 99.

USE, experience; III. iv. 143.

USING, cherishing, entertaining; III. ii. 10.
UTTERANCE; 'to the u.', *i.e. à outrance* = to the uttermost; III. i. 72.

VANTAGE, opportunity; I. ii. 31.
VERITY, truthfulness; IV. iii. 92.
VISARDS, masks; III. ii. 34.
VOUCH'D, assured, warranted; III. iv. 34.

WANT; 'cannot w.', can help; III. vi. 8.
WARRANT IN, justification for; II. iii. 151
WARRANTED, justified; IV. iii. 137.
WASSAIL, revelry; I. vii. 64.
WATCHING, waking; V. i. 12.
WATER-RUG, a kind of poodle; III. i. 94.
WEAL, land, commonwealth; III. iv. 76
WHAT, who; IV. iii. 49.
WHAT IS, *i.e.* what is the time of; III. iv. 126.
WHEN 'TIS, *i.e.* 'when the matter is effected'; II. i. 25.
WHETHER (monosyllabic); I. iii. 111.
WHICH, who; V. i. 66.
WHILE THEN, till then; III. i. 44.
WHISPERS, whispers to; IV. iii. 210.
WHOLESOME, healthy; IV. iii. 105.
WITH, against; IV. iii. 90.
——, by; III. 1. 63.
——, on; IV. ii. 32.
WITHOUT, outside; III. iv. 14.
——, beyond; III. ii. 11, 12.
WITNESS, testimony, evidence; II. ii. 47.
WORM, small serpent; III. iv. 29.
WOULD, should; I. vii. 34.
WRACK, ruin; I. iii. 51

WROUGHT, agitated; I. iii. 149.

YAWNING PEAL, a peal which lulls to sleep; III. ii. 43.
YESTY, foaming; IV. i. 53.
YET, in spite of all, notwithstanding; IV. iii. 69.

Notes

I. i. 1. Perhaps we should follow the punctuation of the Folio, and place a note of interrogation after '*again*'.

I. i. 11. 'Fair is ... Is fair' = What is good is evil and what is evil is good.

I. i. 12. 'filthy air' = the atmosphere clouded by the effects of a thunderstorm.

I. ii. 14. '*damned quarrel*'; Johnson's, perhaps unnecessary, emendation of Ff., '*damned quarry*' (cp. IV. iii. 206); but Holinshed uses 'quarrel' in the corresponding passage.

I. ii. 18. 'smoked with bloody execution' = blood steaming following death.

I. ii. 20–21. Many emendations and interpretations have been advanced for this passage; Koppel's explanation (*Shakespeare Studien*, 1896) is as follows:—'he faced the slave, who never found time for the preliminary formalities of a duel, *i.e.* shaking hands with and bidding farewell to the opponent'; seemingly, however, '*which*' should have '*he*' (*i.e.* Macbeth) and not '*slave*' as its antecedent.

I. ii. 22. 'Till he unseam'd him from the nave to the chaps' = ... cleaved him open from the navel to the jaw.

I. ii. 27–28. 'So from that spring ... / Discomfort swells' = At the point of victory, there is further cause for concern.

I. ii. 33–34. 'Dismay'd not this / Our captains, Macbeth and Banquo?' = Did our leaders Macbeth and Banquo feel dismay?

I. ii. 37. 'As cannons overcharged with double cracks' = Like cannons loaded with double charges of gunpowder.

I. ii. 55. 'Confronted him with self-comparisons' = Matched him in equal combat

I. iii. 2. 'killing swine'. Witches were believed to slaughter livestock and domestic pets.

I. iii. 9. 'And, like a rat without a tail, I'll do, I'll do, and I'll do'. The witch intends to turn herself into a strange creature and take her revenge.

I. iii. 14–17. 'I myself have all the other ... I' the shipman's card' = I control the winds and I know the ports they blow on from all directions of the compass.

I. iii. 15. '*And the very ports they blow*'; Johnson conj. '*various*' for '*very*'; Pope reads '*points*' for '*ports*'; Clar. Press edd. '*orts*': '*blow*'='blow upon'.

I. iii. 22. 'Weary se'nnights nine times nine' = Weary for seven nights a week multiplied by nine times nine. [Nine was considered a magical number.]

I. iii. 32. *'weird'*; Ff., *'weyward'* (prob.=*'weird'*); Keightley, *'weyard'*.

I. iii. 42–43. 'Live you? or are you aught / That man may question?' = Are you alive? Or are you anything capable of being questioned?

I. iii. 55–57. 'You greet ... rapt withal' = You give predictions of such good fortune, or noble futures and royal hopes, that he [Macbeth] appears entranced.

I. iii. 84. 'insane root' – Hallucinatory plant

I. iii. 92–93. 'His wonders ... or his' = He does not know whether his imagination and his celebrations belong to you or him.

I. iii. 96. 'Nothing afeard of what thyself didst make' = You were not afraid of what you yourself were creating [i.e. 'Strange images of death'; line 97].

I. iii. 97–98. *'As thick as hail Came post'*; Rowe's emendation; Ff. read *'As thick as tale Can post'*.

I. iii. 108–09. 'why do you dress me / In borrow'd robes?' = Why do you make me wear another man's clothes?

I. iii. 120. 'trusted home' = completely believed.

I. iii. 123–25. 'oftentimes ... deepest consequence' = Often the forces of evil bring us to harm by telling us truths, winning us over with inaccurate trivialities while misleading us on great matters.

I. iii. 139–42. 'My thought ... what is not' – Murder is for now just a thought, but I am so shaken by it that I am incapable of action, and the only reality is my thoughts.

I. iii. 145–46. 'Like our strange garments ... with the aid of use' = In the way that our new clothes don't fit us properly until they have been worn in.

I. iv. 11–12. 'There's no art / To find the mind's construction in the face' = It's impossible to tell what's going on in a person's mind from his face.

I. iv. 16–18. 'thou art so far before ... overtake thee' – Your worth to me is so far ahead that however I try to reward you, I cannot catch you up.

I. iv. 18–20. 'Would thou ... been mine!' = If only you deserved less, I could repay you in the manner you deserve.

I. iv. 26–27. 'Which do ... love and honour' = They do only what they should, protecting you and so deserving your love and honour.

I. iv. 30–31. 'That hast no ... have done so' = You have deserved this much and it must also be recognized equally.

I. iv. 32–33. 'There if I grow, / The harvest is your own' = If I flourish there, it will add to your benefit.

I. iv. 39–40. 'which honour ... invest him only' = He is not the only one to receive honour.

I. iv. 44. 'The rest is labour, which is not used for you' = My efforts are mere chores if they are not given to you.

I. iv. 48–49. 'that is a ... or else o'erleap' = Malcolm is an obstacle that I will either trip over or jump over.

I. iv. 52–53. 'The eye wink at the hand ... to see ' = The eye will not look at what the hand performs; but let it happen, what the eye fears seeing when the deed is done.

I. v. 15. 'Lay it to thy heart' = Keep it hidden in your heart.

I. v. 19. 'To catch the nearest way' = ... opt for the most direct route of action.

I. v. 21–22. 'what thou wouldst highly, / That wouldst thou holily' = You desire great things attained by fair means.

I. v. 22–23. 'wouldst not play false, / And yet wouldst wrongly win' = You don't want to cheat yet you are prepared to win by unfair means.

I. v. 24–26. The difficulty of these lines arises from the repeated words 'that which' in line 25, and some editors have consequently placed the inverted commas after 'undone'; but 'that which' is probably due to the same expression in the previous line, and we should perhaps read 'and that's which' or 'and that's what'.

I. v. 25–26. 'And that which ... should be undone' = You are more afraid of performing the deed than want it not to be done.

I. v. 42. 'unsex me' = take away my femininity.

I. v. 46–48. 'That no compunctious ... effect and it' = So no natural compassion diverts me from my ruthless purpose, and prevent me from carrying it out.

I. v. 64–65. 'To beguile the time, / Look like the time' = To deceive the present moment, model your behaviour to what is happening in the present moment.

I. v. 70–71. 'Which shall to ... sway and masterdom' = Which is to ensure that the future is given to our royal power and control.

I. vi. 4. 'martlet'; Rowe's emendation of Ff., 'Barlet'.

I. vi. 5. 'loved mansionry'; Theobald's emendation of Ff., 'loved mansonry'; Pope (ed. 2), 'loved masonry'.

I. vi. 4–6. 'The temple-haunting martlet ... wooingly here' = The church dwelling house martin proves by his nest-building that the air is perfect here.

I. vi. 6. '*jutty, frieze*'; Pope, '*jutting frieze*'; Staunton conj. '*jutty, nor frieze,*' &c.

I. vi. 6–8. 'no jutty, frieze ... procreant cradle' – There is no projection, frieze, buttress or other useful spot where the bird will not build its dangling nest, a cradle for its young.

I. vi. 9. '*most*'; Rowe's emendation of Ff., '*must*'; Collier MS., '*much*'.

I. vii. 6. '*shoal*'; Theobald's emendation of Ff. 1, 2, '*schoole*'.

I. vi. 11–12. 'The love that follows ... thank as love' = Love can sometimes be a burden, even though we are thankful for it.

I. vi. 12–14. 'Herein I teach ... your trouble' = I am showing you how to ask God to reward you for your efforts, and therefore you should thank us for imposing on you.

I. vi. 25–28. 'Your servants ever ... your own' = Your subjects are ever yours, and they have their own servants, and all they own is accounted for, for auditing when the king so chooses.

I. vii. 9–10. 'Bloody instructions ... the inventor' = The lessons in murder, once taught, come back to haunt the doer with consequences.

I. vii. 34–35. 'Which would be worn ... so soon' = Which should be enjoyed while they are new, not quickly rejected.

I. vii. 36–38. 'hath it slept ... so freely?' = Has it been asleep, but now wakes feeling ill from a hangover, regretting things said when drunk?

I. vii. 45. '*Like the poor cat i' the adage*'; 'The cat would eat fyshe, and would not wet her feete,' Heywood's *Proverbs*; the low Latin form of the same proverb is:—

'*Catus amat pisces, sed non vult tingere plantas*'.

I. vii. 47. '*do more*'; Rowe's emendation of Ff., '*no more*'.

II. i. 51. '*sleep*'; Steevens conj. '*sleeper,*' but no emendation is necessary; the pause after '*sleep*' is evidently equivalent to a syllable.

I. vii. 70–72. 'what not put ... our great quell?' =We can place the blame on the drunken guards, who will take the blame for our great act.

I. vii. 77. 'Who dares receive it other' = Who would dare to make it otherwise?

II. i. 7–9. 'Merciful powers ... in repose!' = Heavenly powers, guard me against the evil dreams that nature brings forth in sleep.

II. i. 17–19. 'Being unprepared ... free have wrought' = Because we did not have time to prepare, we are unable to entertain in the way we would have desired.

II. i. 26. 'If you shall cleave to my consent, when 'tis' = If you obey me when the time comes.

II. i. 36–37. 'Art thou not ... to sight?' = Deadly vision, can you be held physically as well as seen?

II. i. 44–45. 'Mine eyes ... all the rest' = My eyes are unreliable compared to the other senses, or they are more reliable than the rest.

II. i. 48–49. 'It is the bloody business which informs/Thus to mine eyes' The idea of murder is distorting my vision.

II. i. 55. *'Tarquin's ravishing strides'*; Pope's emendation; Ff., *'Tarquins ravishing sides'*.

II. i. 56. *'sure'*; Pope's conj., adopted by Capell; Ff. 1, 2, *'sowre'*.

II. i. 57. *'which way they walk'*; Rowe's emendation; Ff., *'which they may walk'*.

II. i. 58–59. 'Thy very stones ... suits with it' = Even the stones prattle about where I am, and break the tension and horror of the present time.

II. i. 61. 'Words to the heat of deeds too cold breath gives' = Too much talk will cool the intention to act.

II. ii. 8. 'That death and nature... live or die' = They hover between life and death, and death and nature struggle over their fate.

II. ii. 11–12. 'the attempt and not the deed / Confounds us' = It could be that the unsuccessful attempt and not the deed will ruin us.

II. ii. 35–36. There are no inverted commas in the Folios. The arrangement in the text is generally followed (similarly, II. 42–43).

II. ii. 73. 'To know my deed, 'twere best not know / myself.' = To know what I have done makes it better for me to be lost in absent thoughts.

II. iii. 3–4. 'Here's a farmer, that hanged himself on th' expectation of plenty' – A proverbial reference to a farmer who stored corn to sell at a high profit during a time of scarcity, but who killed himself in despair when there was a good harvest.

II. iii. 17. 'here you may roast your goose' = Do what you need to do. See also Glossary for goose.

II. iii. 34–40. 'therefore much drink ... leaves him.' = Too much drink pulls a man's lust in different directions. It generates lust and quashes it; it turns him on and turns him off; it encourages and dissuades; makes him ready for sex but incapable of action; ultimately it tricks him into sleep and leaves him there.

II. iii. 54. 'The labour we delight in physics pain' = The work we enjoy doing treats the effort of doing it.

II. iii. 72–74. 'Most sacrilegious murder ... life o' the building' = Desecrating murder has broken into the temple of the Lord's anointed king, and stolen the life from it.

II. iii. 90–91. 'The repetition ... murder as it fell' = Recounting what I have said to a woman would kill her as she heard it.

II. iii. 100–01. 'The wine of life ...to brag of' = The wine of life has been drunk and only the dregs are left to brag over.

II. iii. 125–26. 'Why do we ... claim this argument for ours?' = Why don't we speak when this matter pertains to us so significantly?

II. iii. 127–28. 'What should be ... may rush, and seize us?' = What should be said here, as someone could be hidden watching us, and might rush out and take us?

II. iii. 147–49. 'This murderous shaft ... avoid the aim' = The murderous arrow is still in flight, therefore we should avoid its intended aiming point.

II. iv. 28–29. 'Thriftless ambition ... Thine own life's means!' = A wanton ambition that will eat up the very means of your sustenance.

III. i. 34–35. 'When therewithal ... Craving us jointly' = Then the matters of our state require our joint attention.

III. i. 50–51. 'in his royalty ... would be fear'd' = In his regal bearing is that which causes us concern.

III. i. 63–64. 'Thence to be wrench'd ... mine succeeding' = Taken by someone else, not from my own descendant, my son.

III. i. 83. 'To half a soul and to a notion crazed' = To a half-wit and a crazed apprehension.

III. i. 100–01. 'Particular addition ... them all alike' = A special addition to the category 'dog'.

III. i. 107. 'Who wear our health but sickly in his life' = Whose health is fragile in this life.

III. i. 116–19. 'in such bloody distance ... my near'st of life' = He is at sword-fighting distance, so every minute he is alive threatens my own life.

III. i. 130. *'you with the perfect spy o' the time'*; Johnson conj. *'you with a'*; Tyrwhitt conj. *'you with the perfect spot, the time'*; Beckett conj. *'you with the perfectry o' the time'*; Grant White, from Collier MS., *'you, with a perfect spy, o' the time'*; Schmidt interprets *'spy'* to mean 'an advanced guard; that time which will precede the time of the deed, and indicate that it is at hand'; according to others 'spy' = the person who gives the information; the simplest explanation is, perhaps, 'the exact spying out of the time,' *i.e.* 'the moment on't,' which in the text follows in apposition.

III. ii. 4. 'Nought's had ... without content' = Nothing is gained and all is lost when we get what we want and it does not bring contentment.

III. ii. 11–12. 'Things without all remedy / Should be without regard' = Matters that cannot be changed should be ignored.

III. ii. 20. '*our peace*'; so F. 1; Ff. 2, 3, 4, '*our place*'.

III. ii. 33–34. 'Unsafe the while ... flattering streams' = At present we are unsafe, so we must use our position to flatter others.

III. iii. 2. 'He needs not our mistrust ... the direction just' = Don't mistrust him, as he has told us what we need to do, according to Macbeth's directions.

III. iii. 20–21. 'We have lost / Best half of our affair' = We have performed only half of our task.

III iv. 14. "*Tis better thee without than he within*'; probably '*he*' instead of '*him*' for the sake of effective antithesis with '*thee*'; unless, as is possible, '*he within*' = 'he in this room'.

III. iv. 27. 'The least a death to nature' = Any of the wounds would kill.

III. iv. 40. 'Here had we now our country's honour roof'd' = Here is seated the nobility of Scotland under one roof.

III. iv. 42–43. 'Who may I ... pity for mischance!' – I would prefer to confront him for bad manners than pity him for bad luck.

III. iv. 76. 'Ere humane statute purged the gentle weal' – Before humane law cleansed society.

III. iv. 78. '*time has*'; F. 1, '*times has*'; Ff. 2, 3, 4, '*times have*'; the reading of the First Folio is probably what Shakespeare intended.

III. iv. 105–06. '*If trembling I inhabit then*'; various emendations have been proposed, *e.g.* '*I inhibit*,' = '*me inhibit*,' '*I inhibit thee*,' '*I inherit*,' &c.; probably the text is correct, and the words mean 'If I then put on the habit of trembling,' *i.e.* 'if I invest myself in trembling' (*cp.* Koppel, p. 76).

III. iv. 112–13. 'You make me ... that I owe' = You make me strange to myself and my own nature.

III. iv. 119. 'Stand not upon the order of your going' = Don't leave in the correct order of rank.

III. iv. 122. The Folios read:—

> '*It will have blood they say;*
> *Blood will have blood*'.

III. iv. 135–36. 'For mine own ... shall give way' = Everything must be bent for my own good.

III. iv. 143. 'Is the initiate fear that wants hard use' = The fear of an inexperienced person who needs to toughen up.

III. iv. 144. *'in deed'*; Theobald's emendation of Ff., *'indeed'*; Hanmer, *'in deeds'*.

III. v. 13. *'Loves'*; Halliwell conj. *'Lives'*; Staunton conj. *'Loves evil'*.

III. vi. 1–2. 'My former speeches … can interpret farther' = You can draw your own conclusions from what I have said previously.

III. vi. 17–20. 'I do think … so should Fleance' = I believe that if he had had Duncan's sons within reach, which, please God, he never will, they would find out what it is to kill a father, and so would Fleance.

III. vi. 27. *'the most pious Edward,'* i.e. Edward the Confessor.

III. vi. 28–29. 'That the malevolence … his high respect' = Despite the cruelties of fortune, Malcolm is still held in high esteem.

IV. i. 7–8. 'Days and nights … venom sleeping got' = For 30 nights we have collected venom from the sleeping toad.

IV. i. 31. 'Ditch-deliver'd by a drab' = Born of a prostitute in a ditch.

IV. i. 83–84. 'But yet I'll … bond of fate' = I will force fate to deliver on its promise.

IV. i. 97. *'Rebellion's head'*; Theobald's conj., adopted by Hanmer; Ff. read *'Rebellious dead'*; Warburton's conj., adopted by Theobald, *'Rebellious head'*.

IV. i. 121. 'two-fold balls and treble sceptres carry'. In the Scottish coronation

ceremony, the monarch held one orb and one sceptre, whereas the English monarch held one orb and two sceptres. The reference here implies the unification of both English and Scottish crowns, as occurred under James I.

IV. i. 145–46. 'The flighty purpose … go with it' = Plans developed quickly go nowhere unless the action is equally swift.

IV. i. 147–48. 'The very firstlings … of my hand' = From now on my first plans will be those I carry out.

IV. ii. 9. 'He wants the natural touch' = He lacks natural human feelings.

IV. ii. 18. *'when we are traitors And do not know ourselves'*, i.e. when we are accounted traitors, and do not know that we are, having no consciousness of guilt. Hanmer, *'know't o.'*; Keightley, *'know it ourselves'*; but no change seems necessary.

IV. ii. 19–22. 'when we hold … way and move' = Rumour preys on our fears, although it does not know our fears, leaving us adrift as it upon a stormy sea.

IV. ii. 22. *'Each way and move'*; Theobald conj. *'Each way and wave'*; Capell, *'And move each way'*; Steevens conj. *'And each way move'*; Johnson conj. *'Each way, and move—'*; Jackson conj. *'Each wail and moan*'; Ingleby conj. '*Which way we move*'; Anon conj. '*And move each wave*'; Staunton conj. '*Each sway and move*'; Daniel conj. '*Each way it moves*'; Camb. edd. conj. '*Each way and none*'; perhaps '*Each way we move*' is the simplest reading of the words.

IV. ii. 71. '*do worse,*' *i.e.* 'let her and her children be destroyed without warning' (Johnson); (Hanmer, '*do less*'; Capell, '*do less*').

IV. ii. 71–72. 'To do worse ... nigh your person' = Not to warn you would be an act of cruelty, and cruelty is near you.

IV. iii. 14–15. 'but something ... him through me' = You might have seen some of Macbeth's qualities in me'

IV. iii. 15. '*deserve*'; Warburton's emendation, adopted by Theobald; Ff. 1, 2, '*discerne*'; Ff. 3, 4, '*discern*';——, '*and wisdom*'; there is some corruption of text here, probably a line has dropped out. Hanmer reads "*tis wisdom*'; Steevens conj. '*and wisdom is it*'; Collier conj. '*and 'tis wisdom*'; Staunton conj. '*and wisdom 'tis*' or '*and wisdom bids*'; Keightley, '*and wisdom 'twere*'.

IV. iii. 22. 'Angels are bright still, though the brightest fell' = Angels shine bright, although the brightest [Lucifer] fell from heaven.

IV. iii. 28–29. 'Let not my ... mine own safeties' = Do not let my suspicions affront you, as they are necessary for my own safety.

IV. iii. 71–72. 'Convey your pleasures ... may so hoodwink' = If you express your pleasures in secrecy, but appear ordered to the world, you can fool others.

IV. iii. 95–96. 'I have no ... each several crime' = I don't possess them, but rather have many types of evil.

IV. iii. 111. '*Died every day she lived,*' 'lived a life of daily mortification' (Delius).

IV. iii. 127. 'Scarcely have coveted what was mine own' = Barely coveted the things that I already owned.

IV. iii. 142–43. 'their malady ... assay of art' = their illness confounds medical science.

IV. iii. 166–67. 'where nothing ... seen to smile' = Only someone unaware of what is happening can smile.

IV. iii. 175. 'That of an ... the speaker' = Someone who gives news that is just an hour old is criticised for being behind the times.

IV. iii. 235. '*tune*'; Rowe's emendation of Ff., '*time*'.

V. i. 29. '*sense is shut*'; Rowe's emendation of Ff., '*sense are shut*'; S. Walker conj., adopted by Dyce, '*sense' are shut*'. The reading of the Folio probably gives the right reading, 'sense' being taken as a plural.

V. ii. 4–5. 'grim alarm … mortified man' = The call to arms would rouse the dead.

V. ii. 18–19. 'Now minutely revolts … only in command' = Every minute there are new revolts, and people only follow him because of his orders.

V. iii. 1. '*them*,' *i.e.* the thanes.

V. iii. 21. '*cheer*'; Percy conj., adopted by Dyce, '*chair*': ——; '*disseat*', Jennens and Capell conj., adopted by Steevens; F. 1, '*dis-eate*'; Ff. 2, 3, 4, '*disease*'; Bailey conj. '*disseize*'; Daniel conj. '*defeat*'; Furness, '*dis-ease*'; Perring conj. '*disheart*'.

V. iii. 22. '*way of life*'; Johnson proposed the unnecessary emendation '*May of life,*' and several editors have accepted the conjecture.

V. iii. 38. 'As she is troubled with thick-coming fancies' = She is wracked with constant delusions.

V. iii. 44. '*stuff'd*'; Ff. 2, 3, 4, '*stuft*'; Pope, '*full*'; Steevens conj., adopted by Hunter, '*foul*'; Anon conj. '*fraught*', '*press'd*'; Bailey conj. '*stain'd*'; Mull conj. '*steep'd*': ——; '*stuff*'; so Ff. 3, 4; Jackson conj. '*tuft*'; Collier (ed. 2), from Collier MS., '*grief*'; Keightley, '*matter*'; Anon conj. '*slough*', '*freight*'; Kinnear conj. '*fraught*'.

V. iii. 55. '*senna*'; so F. 4; F. 1, '*Cyme*'; Ff. 2, 3, '*Caeny*'; Bulloch conj. '*sirrah*'.

V. iii. 58. '*it*,' *i.e.* the armour.

V. iii. 62. 'Profit again should hardly draw me here' = The lure of payment would not drag me back here.

V. iv. 6–7. 'and make discovery/Err in report of us' = Confuse the reporting of spies.

V. iv. 9–10. 'endure / Our setting down before't' = Will not prevent our laying siege to the castle.

V. iv. 14–15. 'Let our just … the true event' = Let us see if our predictions are fulfilled in the battle.

V. iv. 19. 'Thoughts speculative their unsure hopes relate' = Guesses can generate false hopes.

V. v. 5–6. 'Were they not … beard to beard' = If they hadn't been reinforced with soldiers who should have been on our side, we would have been able to fight them confidently, face to face.

V. v. 14–15. 'Direness, familiar … once start me' = Horror is a familiar element within my bloody thoughts, and no longer disturbs me.

V. v. 43–44. 'To doubt the … lies like truth' = I doubt the lies of the Devil, which sound like truth.

V. v. 47–48. 'If this which … nor tarrying here' = If that which he has predicted comes true, it doesn't make a difference whether we flee or wait here.

V. vii. 1–2. 'They have tied … fight the course'. Bears were tied to stakes prior to being baited by dogs.

V. vii. 15. 'If thou be'st … stroke of mine' = If you are killed but not by my sword.

V. vii. 21–22. 'By this great … Seems bruited' = The loud noise suggests the arrival of a great figure.

V. viii. 2–3. 'whiles I see lives … better upon them' = As long as enemy soldiers are alive, then it is better that I inflict injuries upon them [rather than on himself, as implied in the previous line].

V. viii. 10–11. 'With thy keen … on vulnerable crests' = Your sharp sword is as much use slashing at thin air as attempting to make me bleed, and you would be better bringing it down on weaker heads.

V. viii. 19–20. 'And be these … a double sense' = Don't believe these equivocating fiends any more, who trick us with double meanings.

V. viii. 53. 'They say he parted well and paid his score' = They say he died like a man and did his duty.

V. viii. 49. 'And so his knell is knoll'd' = The bell announcing his death has been rung.

V. viii. 55. 'I see thee compass'd with thy kingdom's pearl' = I see you wearing the crown of Scotland.

WILLIAM SHAKESPEARE —
HIS LIFE AND TIMES

We have few details of Shakespeare's personal life, and some of these are disputed, but we can trace his life in theatre with some confidence. This was a man who learned his craft; insisted on fair remuneration; found (and retained) royal favour and escaped political snares. Aligned with one company, he could write with specific actors in mind and experiment as different theatres offered new staging possibilities. His creativity was impacted only by frequent outbreaks of plague, which closed the theatres.

1557

John Shakespeare marries Mary Arden. The couple may have known each other since childhood; his father farmed land owned by her father.

26 APRIL 1564

The couple's third child, William, is baptised. His date of birth is not known, and the day usually celebrated — 23 April, or Saint George's Day — appeals only because this is known to be the day of his death, in 1616. That said, baptism was expected during this period to take place no later than seven days after birth.

EDUCATION

William is probably educated at the King's New School in Stratford-upon-Avon, about a quarter-mile from his home.

At this time, a grammar school education involves principally the teaching of Latin (with some Greek), preparing boys for careers in the civil service. The art of rhetoric teaches them how to communicate with an audience, learning the importance of delivery and gesture.

Boys also study classical poetry and drama, and write their own compositions, in both English and Latin or Greek. They perform these in front of their class — and sometimes perform plays on holidays.

JULY 1575, KENILWORTH

The Earl of Leicester's Men, a major acting company, perform *The Delivery of the Lady of the Lake* at Kenilworth Castle. Crowds flock to their performances, from 9 to 27 July, and it is possible that William is among them. A reference to 'Arion on the dolphin's back' in *Twelfth Night* (I. ii. 15) may reflect his familiarity with the classical tale, but it may also echo a particularly noteworthy spectacle: musicians performing inside a dolphin

27 NOVEMBER 1582

A marriage licence is issued to William, then aged 18, and Anne Hathaway, then aged 26. It's probable the marriage is one of necessity: permission is granted to read the marriage banns only once (not the usual three times) and a daughter, Susanna, is baptised less than six months later, on 26 May 1583.

2 FEBRUARY 1585

Twins, son Hamnet and daughter Judith, are baptised.

1585–1592, THE 'LOST YEARS'

William disappears from the historical record, and we do not know how he supports his young family during this time. Is he a schoolmaster? A legal clerk? A soldier?

At some point in the late 1880s, he arrives in London. Perhaps to avoid prosecution for poaching deer – though probably not. This and other stories arise in the years (and centuries) following his death, in part a response to misreading contemporary documents. 'Shakespeare' is a common enough name in the sixteenth century, and there is only one document that seems certain to refer to William: a 'complaints bill' for a case before the Queen's Bench between 1588 and 1589.

SHAKESPEARE, THE ACTOR

William begins his life in the theatre as an actor. This aspect of his life is often overlooked, not least because actors are held in low esteem during his lifetime – and, indeed, for many centuries after it.

Reform of the Poor Laws during Elizabeth's reign had made life for travelling companies particularly difficult. An act 'for the punishment of vagabondes' (1572) allowed for the arrest and imprisonment of the unemployed, and itinerant actors were often targeted. Acting companies therefore required the protection of theatrical sponsors such as the Earl of Leicester and the Earl of Sussex, whose playing company the young William joins.

Though never a star, he will act for 15 years — which suggests a certain skill. At a time when audiences are both loud and generous with their responses, a bad player will be hissed from the stage, their exit further encouraged by the lobbing of an orange or two. His first biographer, Nicolas Rowe, tells us that his role as the Ghost in *Hamlet* was 'the top of his performance'. William also appears in the cast list for several plays by Ben Jonson, including *Sejanus*, performed in 1603.

1589–1592, EARLY WRITING

Apparently recognizing that he does not excel as an actor, William finds a new role: he breathes new life into old and tired plays, collaborates with established dramatists and begins to write alone.

With others, he writes: *The Second Part of Henry the Sixth* (1591); *The Third Part of Henry the Sixth* (1591); *The Lamentable Tragedy of Titus Andronicus* (1592); and *The First Part of Henry the Sixth* (1592).

On his own, he writes the following plays (whose dates are difficult to establish with any certainty): *The Taming of the Shrew* (1589–92); *The Two Gentleman of Verona* (1591–2); and *King Richard the Third* (1592/4). Lord Strange's Men are associated with the first performance of this last play, and Lord Strange himself is a direct descendant of Thomas Stanley, a character in the play whose role is pivotal. William may be a member of the company.

1592, 'AN UPSTART CROW'

Robert Greene, a popular dramatist, publishes a pamphlet, *Greenes, Groats-worth of Witte, bought with a million of Repentance*. He has both a BA and an MA from Cambridge, and complains:

> there is an upstart Crow, beautified with our feathers, that with his Tygers hart wrapt in a Players hyde, supposes he is as well able to bombast out a blanke verse as the best of you: and being an absolute Johannes fac totum, is in his owne conceit the onely Shake-scene in a countrey.

This *Johannes fac totum* is a Jack of all trades – and, obviously, a master of none. Drama should clearly be left to university graduates, not actors.

Just six years later, however, another Cambridge graduate, the author Francis Meres, will write:

> As Plautus and Seneca are accounted the best for comedy and tragedy among the Latins, so Shakespeare among the English is the most excellent in both kinds for the stage.

Incidentally, the reference to 'his Tygers hart wrapt in a Players hyde' is an allusion to a line from *Henry VI, Part III* — which suggests the play had enjoyed considerable success.

1593–94

Plague closes the theatres, and Lord Strange's Men leave London to tour. William writes two narrative poems, which prove popular and will be reprinted several times during his lifetime. He dedicates both to Henry Wriothesley, 3rd Earl of Southampton. The dedication for Venus and Adonis is brief – 'The love I dedicate to your Lordship is without end'; the dedication for *The Rape of Lucrèce* is extravagant:

> The love I dedicate to your lordship is without end ... What I have done is yours; what I have to do is yours; being part in all I have, devoted yours.

We do not know the nature of the relationship between the two men, and both dedications offer few clues – during this period, writers depend on their sponsors for support, political as well as financial. However, the Earl is often identified as the 'Fair Youth' of Shakespeare's sonnets: his celebrated looks and personality seem to match.

It's an identification that is disputed, not least because Henry is 39 (hardly a youth) when the sonnets are first published, in 1609 — though this is a collection written between 1593 and 1608.

1594, *THE COMEDY OF ERRORS*

William adapts *Menaechmi*, by Plautus — a play he may well have read at school. It is performed by 'a company of base and common fellows' at Gray's Inn Hall on 28 December 1594.

1594, THE LORD CHAMBERLAIN'S MEN

Many members of Lord Strange's Men leave to found this 'playing company', under the patronage of Henry Carey, 1st Baron Hunsdon and the Lord Chamberlain. It will become known as the King's Men in 1603, when the new king, James I, becomes patron.

Profits (and debts) are split between eight 'sharers', including William and Richard Burbage, who will become one of the most famous actors of his time and the first to play the roles of Hamlet, Othello, King Lear and Macbeth.

With this new arrangement, William effectively receives royalties for his work, at a time when writers are usually at the mercy of theatre managers, earning low prices and paid only according to the amount

produced. In 1600, the impresario Philip Henslowe is paying £6–7 a
play and the proceeds from one day's performance.

Originally the company performs at The Theatre, Shoreditch. On 29
December 1598, after difficulties with the landlord and a move to
another theatre, The Theatre is dismantled overnight and carried south of
the river to Southwark, where a new theatre is built: The Globe.

1595–1596

The Lord Chamberlain's Men have exclusive rights to perform
William's plays, which gives him an unusual opportunity — to
develop roles for and in collaboration with the actors.

> • *Love's Labour's Lost*
> Probably written around this time, the play is unusual for having
> no clear literary source while its pageants recall royal
> entertainments. (It will be performed in front of the Queen at
> Christmas, 1597.)
> Does the play have a sequel, *Love's Labour's Won*? Francis Meres
> suggests as much, but it's not certain whether this is a play that has
> now been lost or is simply an alternative title to another play.

> • *A Midsummer Night's Dream*
> This may be the first play William writes for the Lord
> Chamberlain's Men — though the first certain date we have for its
> performance is 1604 at Hampton Court. Bottom may have been
> played by the great comic actor Will Kempe.

> • *The Tragedy of Romeo and Juliet*
> According to the First Quarto, published in 1597, this play 'hath
> been often (and with great applause) plaid publiquely' — which
> suggests it is an immediate success. Richard Burbage probably
> plays Romeo, and a misprint in the First Quarto suggests that Will
> Kempe plays Peter.

> • *The Life and Death of King Richard the Second*
> It's possible that William plays the role of John of Gaunt. The play
> is popular and will be printed three times by 1598.

11 AUGUST 1596

Son Hamnet is buried, dead from unknown causes at the age of 11.

1597–1598

Throughout his career, William moves between London and Stratford, where he buys New Place as his family home, in 1597. It is one of the largest properties in the town, which suggests he has enjoyed considerable financial success.

By 1598, he has also secured a reputation: his name is now a selling point and appears on the title pages of editions of his plays.

• *The Merchant of Venice*
Richard Burbage plays Shylock and Will Kempe plays Lancelot Gobbo, in a play described by Francis Meres and the First Folio as a comedy. It has been performed 'divers times' by 1600, the date of a first edition.

• *The First Part of Henry the Fourth*
The character we know now as Falstaff is originally called Oldcastle. This proves controversial: Oldcastle's descendants, the Lords Cobham, are powerful and take advantage when Henry Carey, the Lord Chamberlain, dies. The company is now 'piteously persecuted by the Lord Mayor and the aldermen', according to the contemporary playwright Thomas Nashe. Within the year, the appointment of Carey's son to Lord Chamberlain restores the company's protection, and Oldcastle is renamed Falstaff.

• *The Second Part of Henry the Fourth*
The epilogue thanks the audience and assures them that Sir John Falstaff will return in a new play. It also clarifies that Falstaff is not Oldcastle, who 'died martyr, and this is not the man'.

• *Much Ado About Nothing*
The most performed of Shakespeare's comedies, it is very popular in the years following its first performance. Will Kempe plays Dogberry, who will leave the company in 1599 — possibly because his talent for improvisation proves irritating. *Hamlet* (written within the next two years) includes this advice to the Players: 'And let those that play your clowns speak no more than is set down for them'.

1599

• *The Life of Henry the Fifth*
In the final act, Henry's triumphant return from London is compared to the Earl of Essex, soon to be 'from Ireland coming, / Bringing rebellion broached on his sword'. It's a confident prediction for the Queen's favourite, but by June England knows that his expedition has failed: the new play is already out of date.

• *As You Like It*
Scholars agree that this is the first play to be performed at the
Globe. Tradition has it that William plays Adam, who may have
written the role of Rosalind with a specific boy player in mind.

• *The Tragedy of Julius Caesar*
Richard Burbage plays the role of Brutus. Caesar is played by the
actor John Heminges, who will be co-editor of the First Folio.

1600–01

• *The Tragedy of Hamlet*
Richard Burbage is the first to play the Prince. Many believe that
John Heminges plays Polonius, and that contemporary audiences
laugh at the boastful line: 'I did enact Julius Caesar: I was killed i'
the Capitol; Brutus killed me'.

• *The Merry Wives of Windsor*
A play that shows signs of having been written in haste.
Biographer Nicolas Rowe insists that the Queen 'was so well
pleased with that admirable character of *Falstaff*, in the two parts
of *Henry the Fourth*, that she commanded him [Shakespeare] to
continue it for one play more, and to shew him in love'. It's a
story that has as many detractors as supporters.

• *Twelfth Night, or What You Will*
Whether or not this is commissioned to perform during Twelfth
Night celebrations at Whitehall Palace in 1601, the comedy is
written around this time. Robert Arnim has replaced Will Kempe as
the leading comic actor, and William is now writing for him: Feste
is a character who is no mere entertainer but shows a keen
intelligence.

1603–1610

Repeated outbreaks of plague close theatres (for a total of 60 months
– five full years), and William's output slows.

He collaborates several times with Thomas Middleton, who also
contributes scenes to Macbeth, and with George Wilkins for *Pericles,
Prince of Tyre* (1608). The Tragedy of Cymbeline (1610) also shows
signs of collaboration.

In Thomas North's translation of *Plutarch's Lives* (first published in
1580, then expanded in 1595 and again in 1603), he finds inspiration
for *The Tragedy of Antony and Cleopatra* (1607–08) and *Coriolanus*
(1605–08). It's clear he also reads Plutarch's original Greek text closely.

There are no records of performances for *All's Well That Ends Well* (1605) or *The Life of Timon of Athens* (1605), which may never have been produced.

• *The Tragedy of Othello* (1604)
Richard Burbage plays the Moor. It is possible that Robert Arnim plays Iago: he was the actor most usually given songs, and Iago sings two drinking songs. The historical setting – the Turkish invasion of Cyprus, leading to the Battle of Lepanto – may be politically astute: a new monarch sits on the throne, James I, and he has recently written a poem about the battle.

• *Measure for Measure* (1604)
This may have been prompted by his research for Othello: an important source for both plays is Cinthio's Gli Hecatommithi.

• *The Tragedy of King Lear* (1605–06)
Richard Arnim plays the Fool, a character who is no clown but who dares to criticize the king even as he remains loyal. Richard Burbage plays Lear, a story with contemporary echoes. In 1603, Sir Brian Annesley, a rich father of three daughters, had become senile. His two older daughters tried to take advantage to contest his will, knowing that his main beneficiary was their younger sister, Cordell.

• *The Tragedy of Macbeth* (1606)
Several details suggest strongly that this play was written in the aftermath of the Gunpowder Plot of 1605. The words 'fair' and 'foul' are the echoes a sermon given by Lancelot Andrewes in front of the king; a medal struck to celebrate the plot's thwarting depicted a serpent hiding among flowers, echoing the advice given by Lady Macbeth: 'Look like the innocent flower, but be the serpent under't'.

1611

• *The Winter's Tale*
The play is based closely on *Pandosto*, by Robert Greene who had been so contemptuous of the 'upstart crow'. Staged at the Globe — the earliest performance recorded is May — it will be performed at Court in front of the King in November.

• *The Tempest*
This seems to have been written for staging at the Blackfriars

playhouse, an indoor theatre owned by the company since 1608. The characters who leave the stage at the end of Act IV are the same who return for Act V. This suggests an interval — probably to replace the candles and torches that provided lighting.

1612–14

William now works with John Fletcher, who will eventually replace him as the company's playwright.

23 APRIL 1616

William dies. The cause is unknown and seems to have been unexpected; he had declared himself to be in 'perfect health' when preparing his will, barely a month earlier. Half a century later, John Ward, vicar of Stratford, will record the local gossip: 'Shakespeare, Drayton, and Ben Jonson had a merry meeting and, it seems, drank too hard, for Shakespeare died of a fever there contracted.'

Three King's Men receive bequests: Richard Burbage, John Heminges and Henry Condell.

13 MARCH 1619

Richard Burbage dies — and London mourns. 'He's gone and with him what a world are dead', writes an anonymous poet, remembering 'Hamlet ... scant of breath', 'Tyrant Macbeth with unwash'd, bloody hand', and 'let me not forget one chiefest part, / Wherein, beyond the rest, he mov'd the heart; / The grieved Moor'.

1623, THE FIRST FOLIO

John Heminges and his fellow King's Man Henry Condell prepare and edit *Mr. William Shakespeare's Comedies, Histories, & Tragedies* for publication. Its significance cannot be underestimated: it is the only reliable text for about 20 plays, and the first publication for a further 18.

The preface tells us that a funerary monument has been erected at Holy Trinity Church, Stratford to honour William Shakespeare, a poet with the genius of Socrates and the art of Virgil: 'The earth buries him, the people mourn him, [Mount] Olympus possesses him'.